THE ILLUMINATED HAFIZ

Also
by Our
Contributors

MICHAEL GREEN

The Illuminated Rumi, with Coleman Barks
One Song: A New Illuminated Rumi
The Illuminated Prayer: The Five-Times Prayer of the Sufis
The Unicornis Manuscripts: On the History and Truth of the Unicorn
Zen & the Art of the Macintosh: Discoveries on the Path to Computer Enlightenment

COLEMAN BARKS

The Essential Rumi
Rumi: Bridge to the Soul
Rumi: The Big Red Book
A Year with Rumi: Daily Readings
The Hand of Poetry: Five Mystic Poets of Persia, with lectures by Hazrat Inayat Khan

ROBERT BLY

Collected Poems
The Angels Knocking on the Tavern Door:
Thirty Poems of Hafez, translated by Bly and Leonard Lewisohn
The Soul Is Here for Its Own Joy: Sacred Poems from Many Cultures
Iron John: A Book about Men
More Than True: The Wisdom of Fairy Tales

MEHER BABA

Discourses
God Speaks: The Theme of Creation and Its Purpose
The Everything and the Nothing
Listen, Humanity
The Path of Love

PETER BOOTH

Dante / Hafiz: Readings on the Sigh, the Gaze, and Beauty, with Franco Masciandaro
The Incomparable Hafiz (forthcoming)

OMID SAFI

Radical Love: Teachings from the Islamic Mystical Tradition
Memories of Muhammad: Why the Prophet Matters
Progressive Muslims: On Justice, Gender, and Pluralism
The Politics of Knowledge in Premodern Islam: Negotiating Ideology and Religious Inquiry

THE ILLUMINATED
HAFIZ

Love Poems for the Journey to Light

Illuminated by Michael *&* Saliha Green

Translations by
Coleman Barks • Robert Bly • Meher Baba • Peter Booth

with Jonathan Granoff
Thomas Rain Crowe • Carl Ernst • Elizabeth T. Gray, Jr. *&* Iraj Anvar
James R. Newell • Annemarie Schimmel • *&* Others
Foreword by Omid Safi
Edited by Nancy Owen Barton

sounds true
BOULDER, COLORADO

Sounds True
Boulder, CO 80306

Published 2019

Printed in South Korea

Library of Congress Cataloging-in-Publication Data

Names: Hafiz, active 14th century, author. | Barks, Coleman, Translator. |Barton, Nancy Owen, editor. | Green, Michael, 1943–
Illustrator. | Green, Saliha, Illustrator.
Title: The Illuminated Hafiz: love poems for the journey to light /translations by Coleman Barks with Robert Bly, Peter
Booth, Omid Safi, Meher Baba, and others; illuminated by Michael and Saliha Green; foreword by Omid Safi; edited by
Nancy Owen Barton.
Description: Boulder, CO: Sounds True, 2019. | Includes bibliographical references and index.
Identifiers: LCCN 2019007963 (print) | LCCN 2019009016 (ebook) | ISBN 9781683644194 (ebook) |
ISBN 9781683643425 (hardback)
Classification: LCC PK6465.Z31 (ebook) | LCC PK6465.Z31 B38 2019 (print) | DDC 808.81—dc23
LC record available at https://lccn.loc.gov/2019007963

10 9 8 7 6 5 4 3 2 1

*N*o one has seen your face
yet you have a thousand protectors.

You are a rose still in a bud
yet a hundred nightingales
sing your praise.

رومی تو کس ندید و هزارت رقیب هست

در غنچه هنوز و صدت عندلیب هست

Although the sun
of the heavens
is the light
of the world,

it is the dust
of Your feet
that gives
the eye of the sun
its brightness.

گرچه خورشید فلک چشم و چراغ عالمست
روشنائی بخش چشم اوست خاک پای تو

Contents

Do not procrastinate!
Start to love this very moment.
Do not forget the Beloved
even for one instant.

Hafiz: The Illuminated Jewel

The collected poetry of Shams al-Din Muhammad Hafiz of Shiraz (d. 1390), known as the *Divan-e Hafiz,* is among the most widely circulated texts in the history of Islam. His honorific name, Hafiz (pronounced HA fez), indicates one who has committed the whole of the Qur'an to heart, a reminder of the intimate relationship between love, mystics, and scripture. Hafiz is the great master of ambiguity, sensuality, and spiritual intoxication, perpetually mindful of the awesome sense of bearing witness to that sacred cosmic bond between humanity and the Divine, a role that is overwhelming, humbling, and, paradoxically, a font of honor.

Jalal al-Din Rumi, Hafiz's renowned predecessor, left behind tens of thousands of lines of poetry, ecstatic and passionate. When reading Rumi, wave after wave of love sweeps us up and carries us back into the Divine Ocean that we have never left. Hafiz's verse is different, if no less impassioned. With Hafiz we get something close to five hundred *ghazals* (love lyrics), each between seven to fourteen lines long, poems so beautifully and perfectly crafted that they resemble exquisite gems whose every facet has been cut by a masterful artist. If Rumi is a tumultuous ocean of love, Hafiz is an illuminated jewel.

> A rose like beauty
> in my embrace.
> Wine
> at hand
> Beloved,
> pleased.
> Next to me
> the sultan of the whole world
> would be a servant.

The intoxication that Hafiz speaks of here is sensual and spiritual all at once, defying any easy categorization. The Persian language has no gender associated with its pronouns, nor any capitalization. Is the beloved that Hafiz speaks of the young man who is pouring the cup of wine? A spiritual teacher? A female beloved? The Prophet? God? It could be any of them, and in a way that only makes sense in the universe of mysticism; it is all of them, all at once. Here is what ambiguity means in the context of Sufi mysticism: It is not that this love is earthly *or* heavenly. It is simply a reminder that all-pervading love erupts out of the Divine, bringing this world into being, illuminates this world, and carries us back to the source. Ultimately, this intoxication is *esqh,* "Radical Love." Hafiz recognizes that love is the divine keepsake, simultaneously the unleashing of God onto this realm, and a reminder of the divine origin of Existence.

Hafiz's relationship with the Divine is tender and subtle. His is not a stern God but more of a perfect lover who draws you closer and closer:

> A secret whisper came to me
> from the Tavern's corner,
> "Drink!
> He forgives."
> God's grace is bigger
> than my sin.

This subtlety and ambiguity makes translating Hafiz a particular challenge. We see this same challenge in translations of Rumi's verse: a tendency to downplay his Muslimness, his embeddedness in the rich universe of Persian literature, and even his religious background. Rumi's thousands of references to God, Muhammad, and the Qur'an are often eliminated and erased in favor of a universal Beloved. This may render Rumi more accessible to a wider audience but does not help us locate him as a Persian-speaking Muslim mystic who seeks to ascend to God in the footsteps of Muhammad and was literally called the "offspring of the soul of Muhammad." In the case of Hafiz, some translations are even more disconnected from the poetry of this fourteenth-century Persian mystic from Shiraz. What's more, many of the hundreds of floating memes and poems that appear on social media bear literally no connection whatsoever to anything that the historical Hafiz ever said. Translating Hafiz's verses properly seems almost impossible, yet they call to be heard in this, and every, age.

This is why I am so grateful for the efforts of Michael and Saliha Green and the others included in these pages in summoning Hafiz here and now in words and images that both faithfully preserve the spirit of his work and open his illuminated love to all, without boundary or prejudice, to—if an intoxication metaphor may be allowed—pour Hafiz's old wine into new skin.

Let us drink, friends, from this masterful poet, this incomparable intoxicated mystic who committed the Qur'an to heart and has become himself an intoxication. Let us drink this love, for the Divine forgives . . .

—Omid Safi, PhD
Durham, NC, 2019

A Mystical Carpet Ride

When we set about illuminating this book, we suspected we might be in for a wild ride—because Hafiz has that kind of reputation. A wild ride it has been, both inside our studio and in the turbulent world outside our door. The title *Love Poems for the Journey to Light* turned out not to be just a lovely spiritual turn of phrase for the jacket. Hafiz is one of the real, God-awakened ones. Once he has been invited into your life, be prepared to head into new, unexplored territory because, as he says, "Love opens from its center."

Hafiz's authentic spirituality doesn't avoid suffering. For us it includes the existential threat of climate change all the way down to the endless hurts that humans inflict on themselves and others. But like the enchanting fragrance of a rose delicately unfolding, we found the beauty of his poems drawing us into a place of deeper truth. It's here that a power can be found greater than all the negative forces in the world rolled together. With Hafiz, this power is boundless Love, or, more intimately, the Beloved.

The poems herein are loosely organized, as much as they can be, along the soul's journey to Light: from the soul's original home we come, traveling through this world of experience, to return once again to Light—as Light. Reading these verses to ourselves and to each other, we feel a little closer to this place where we all truly exist, where the soul lives, and where Light is. "Where there is no other."

As you embark on your own mystical carpet ride with Hafiz in these pages, let the words and images lift your heart and mind. You'll find a host of deeper meanings in Hafiz's words and images in the glossary. The commentaries from our kind contributors offer further context and insight.

Assembling this book involved a lot of serendipity and generosity. The love for Hafiz is without limit! Our preconceived notions were tossed out the window as an unseen presence arranged the images, assembled the contributors, and ordered what needed to be said. We apologize for whatever we got wrong. We are grateful for the many hands that have shaped this volume. May all hearts be free.

In the ghazal, the lyrical form in which Hafiz wrote, it was traditional for the poet to include his pen name in the final couplet with commentary and as a seal of identification. In that spirit, Hafiz must have the last word here. "Peace comes when we are friends together, remembering . . . ."

Michael and Saliha Green
Green Barn Studios, 2019

THERE IS
NO OTHER

Peace comes when we are friends together, remembering.
Hafiz! Your honest desire and your benevolence
free the soul to emerge as what it is.

I CREATED YOU
I KNOW WHAT WHISPERS
IN YOUR SOUL

AND I AM NEARER TO YOU

THAN THE BEATING

OF YOUR OWN HEART

Last night in the radiance

LAST NIGHT I HEARD ANGELS
POUNDING ON THE DOOR
OF THE TAVERN.

THEY HAD KNEADED
THE CLAY OF ADAM,
AND THEY THREW
THE CLAY IN THE SHAPE
OF A WINE CUP.

I AM A NOBODY,
JUST A SQUATTER
SITTING IN THE DUST
OF THE PUBLIC STREET;
AND YET THESE SACRED BEINGS
FROM THE INNERMOST SANCTUARY
DRANK SOME WINE WITH ME.

THE HEAVENS COULD NOT BEAR
THE WEIGHT OF THE TRUST.
WHEN THE LOTS WERE
THROWN AGAIN,
THE TRUST FELL ON MAN,
ON ME, AN IDIOT AND A FOOL.

LET'S FORGIVE
THE SEVENTY- TWO SECTS
FOR THEIR RIDICULOUS WARS
AND MISBEHAVIORS.
BECAUSE THEY COULDN'T ACCEPT
THE PATH OF TRUTH,
THEY TOOK THE ROAD OF MOONSHINE.

THANKS BE TO GOD,
THE DARLING WHOM I LOVE AND I
LIVE IN PEACE. EACH TIME THE PLAYFUL ANGELS
IN PARADISE CATCH SIGHT OF US,
THEY REACH FOR THEIR WINE GLASSES
AND DANCE.

In the cosmology of Persian mystics the descent of man's spirit is represented in an allegory that describes angels, under God's instructions, kneading dust with the wine of God's love over a forty-day period and shaping it into human form—the chalice of the covenant of God's love. It is the metaphorical drinking of the wine of God's love that leads the soul back to its source in God. The Persian mystics call this process the spiritual path. The culmination of this journey is termed God-realization, or Union with God as infinite eternal Love. This is the subject of Hafiz's poetry—his magnificent love poems for our journey to light.

I did not fall away from the mosque

TO THE TAVERN OF RUIN
BY MY OWN WISH.
EVERYTHING THAT HAS HAPPENED TO ME
TOOK PLACE THROUGH SOME AGREEMENT
MADE IN PRE-ETERNITY.

WHAT CAN BE DONE? FOR EACH OF US
WHO HAS FALLEN DOWN INTO TIME,
THE SITUATION IS THE SAME
AS THE NEEDLE FACES
INSIDE THE COMPASS.

THERE IS NO WAY
TO KEEP FROM TURNING.

We are the lords of owning nothing!

BUT WE HAVE
NO TONGUE
TO USE FOR REQUESTS.

IS THERE A NEED FOR APPEAL
WHEN WE'RE ALREADY
WITH THE GENEROUS?

THE SKY-WHEEL TURNS US INTO DAWN
AND FILLS CREATION AGAIN
WITH COLOR.

LET IT BE OUR WEAKNESS, THIS THIRST-LOVE
FOR THE WORLD, THE SUN COMING UP
LIKE RED-GOLD BEING POURED!

THE POTTER'S WHEEL MOVES,
AND SHAPES CHANGE QUICKLY.

LET THE JAR I AM BECOMING
TURN TO A WINE CUP.
FILL ME WITH YOUR LOVE
FOR BEING AWAKE.

I'M NO HYPOCRITE RENUNCIATE.
CALL ME THIS DELICIOUS SUBSTANCE
YOU TASTE WHEN YOU CREATE NEW BEAUTY.

BE STRONG, HAFIZ!
WORK HERE INSIDE TIME,
WHERE WE FAIL, CATCH HOLD
AGAIN, AND CLIMB.

Seek life and patience,
for the great wheel, with its sleight of hand,
has a thousand tricks more strange than these.

This is what the broke drunkard says.

Don't vex me with your contempt.
old friends have certain rights, surely,
more rare than all the jewels you've stashed.

But your face, the wealth
that mirrors the sun and moon.
I can't say its value!

Don't scold me again. Whatever happened
was supposed to happen, wasn't it?

Don't you worry that my breath
may stain your white wool?

Pour me more of that from last night,
so I can forget how much I spent.

And Hafiz! I want to hear *your* songs.
They're the best, I swear it,
by the book inscribed in your chest.

میان عاشق و معشوق هیچ حایل نیست

تو خود حجاب خودی حافظ از میان برخیز

Now that you've ripped open the shirt of their patience,
your lovers will not let go of the hem of your garment.

Between lover and Beloved
there is no veil.
Hafiz, you yourself are the veil.
Get out of the way.

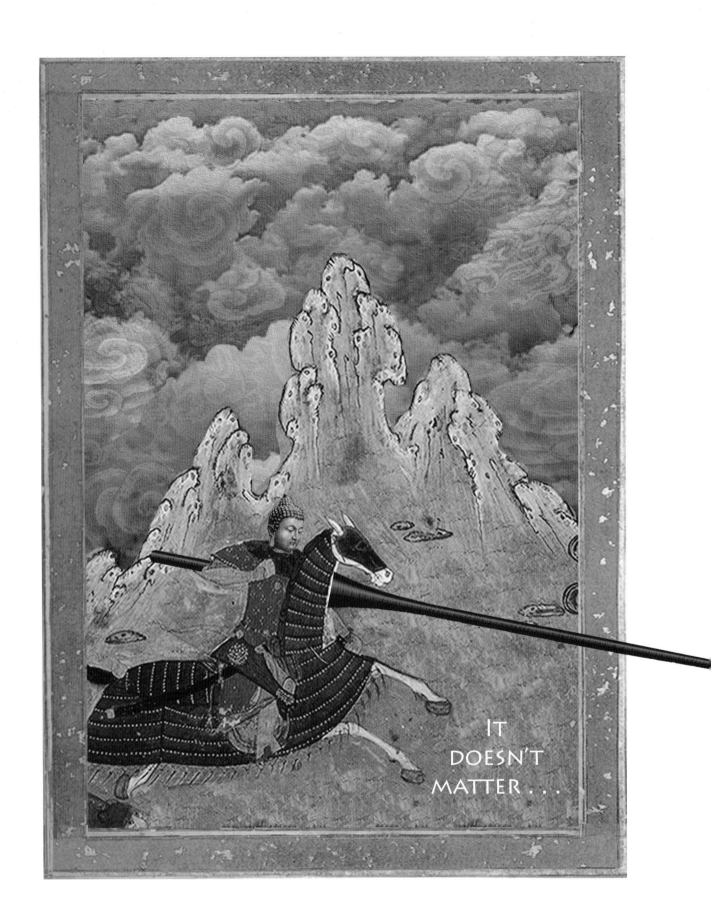

IT
DOESN'T
MATTER . . .

IT DOESN'T MATTER EVERYONE'S AGAINST ME.
  BEING NEAR YOU GIVES LIFE.
    YOUR ABSENCE, DEATH.

      A ROSE TEARS OPENS FROM ITS CENTER.
        WILL I GO TO SLEEP BEFORE YOU ARRIVE?
        IS LONGING ALL THERE IS OF LOVE?

        I WANT YOUR KNIFE MORE
        THAN SOMEONE ELSE'S SALVE.
      LET MY HEAD BE THE LANCE'S TARGET.
    DON'T HOLD BACK THE HORSE,
  AND DON'T VEER OFF!

TIE ME CLOSE WITH THE SADDLE STRAP YOU USE FOR SMALL GAME.

WHEN DUST FROM YOUR DOORSILL IS PUT ON MY HEAD
THEY'LL SAY, *HAFIZ HAS BEEN CROWNED KING!*

I WILL NOT DENY
WHAT I DESIRE.
MY LIPS WANT YOUR LIPS,
NOT A SUBSTITUTE.

I SLEEP WITH MY HEAD
ON *THIS* DOORSILL,
NOT SOME OTHER.

THE GRIEF
OF NEVER HAVING THE PEACE
OF YOUR PRESENCE
MAKES BREATH
ONE LONG SIGH.

WHEN I AM DEAD,
OPEN THE GRAVE

AND WATCH A CLOUD OF SMOKE
RISE AROUND YOUR FEET,

SMOTHERED FIRE-FUMES
FROM MY SHROUD.

Beloved come near!

A lover walks the meadow
looking for flowers. Every man
and every woman
Does this looking
like streams of water
running everywhere together.

Show yourself here
where the pitiful
sit and sing,

where Hafiz's name
comes up, and brings tears.

The holy court of love

IS A THOUSAND TIMES HIGHER
THAN THE HOUSE OF REASON.
ONLY A MAN WHO HOLDS
HIS SOUL LIGHTLY
ON HIS SLEEVE CAN KISS
THE THRESHOLD OF THAT COURT.

I am well-known throughout the whole city
for being a wild-haired lover;
   and I'm that man who has
      never darkened his vision by seeing evil.

Let's be faithful
to what we love;
   let's accept blame
      and keep our spirits high,
      because on our road, being
      hurt by the words of others
      is a form of infidelity.

I said to the master of the tavern:
   "Tell me,
      which is the road of salvation?"
         He lifted his wine and said,

      "Not talking about the faults
         of other people."

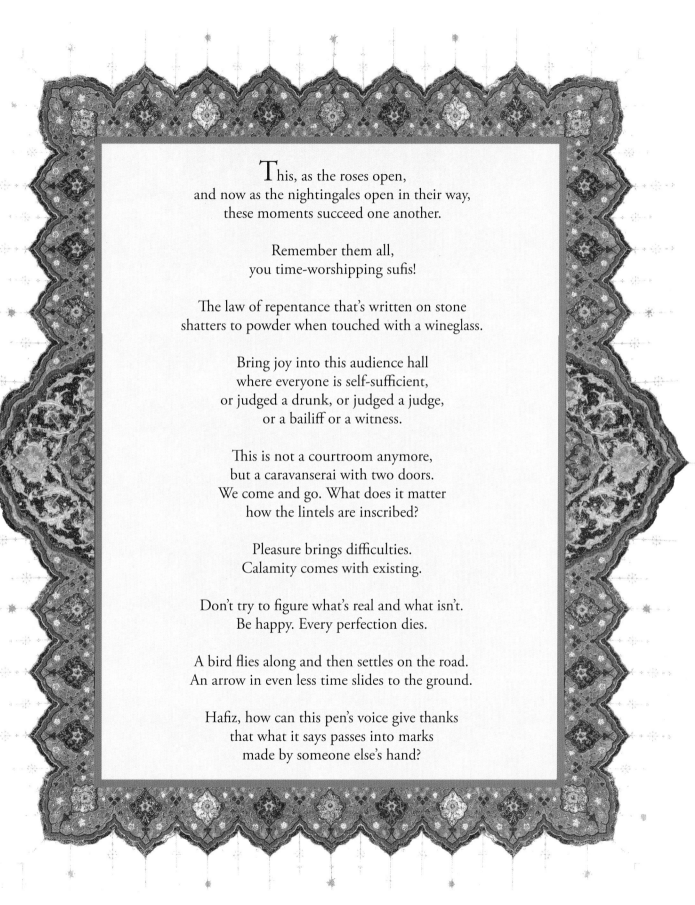

This, as the roses open,
and now as the nightingales open in their way,
these moments succeed one another.

Remember them all,
you time-worshipping sufis!

The law of repentance that's written on stone
shatters to powder when touched with a wineglass.

Bring joy into this audience hall
where everyone is self-sufficient,
or judged a drunk, or judged a judge,
or a bailiff or a witness.

This is not a courtroom anymore,
but a caravanserai with two doors.
We come and go. What does it matter
how the lintels are inscribed?

Pleasure brings difficulties.
Calamity comes with existing.

Don't try to figure what's real and what isn't.
Be happy. Every perfection dies.

A bird flies along and then settles on the road.
An arrow in even less time slides to the ground.

Hafiz, how can this pen's voice give thanks
that what it says passes into marks
made by someone else's hand?

Love seems easy
in a circle of friends,
but it's difficult, difficult.

Morning air through the window,
the taste of it,
with every moment camel bells
leaving the caravanserai.

This is how we wake,
with winespills
on the prayer rug, and even
the tavernmaster is loading up.

My life has gone
from willfulness to disrepute,
and I won't conceal, either, the joy
that led me out toward laughter.

I will ride
on Hafiz's ship
for on
this ocean

it alone has
as cargo
the words
that produce
pearls.

من وسفینهٔ حافظ که جز درین دریا
بضاعت سخن دُرفشان نمی‌بینم

Mountainous Ocean

A MOON HIDDEN BEHIND CLOUDS,
THE TERROR OF BEING DRAWN UNDER.
HOW CAN SOMEONE WITH A LIGHT SHOULDER-PACK
WALKING THE BEACH
KNOW HOW A NIGHT SEA-JOURNEY IS?

HAFIZ! STAY IN THE DANGEROUS LIFE THAT'S YOURS.
THERE YOU'LL MEET

The face that dissolves fear.

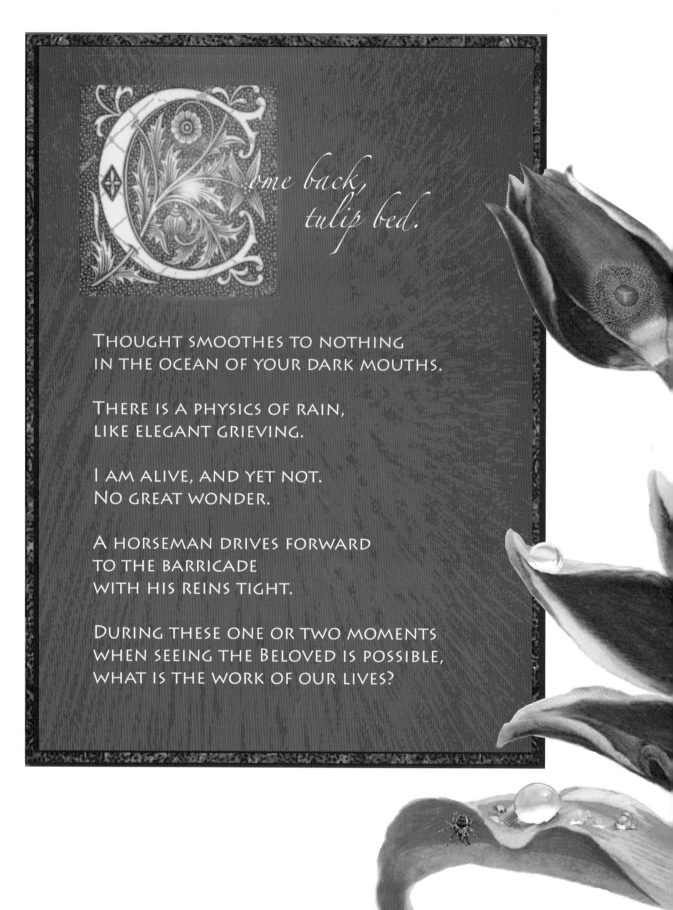

Come back,
tulip bed.

Thought smoothes to nothing
in the ocean of your dark mouths.

There is a physics of rain,
like elegant grieving.

I am alive, and yet not.
No great wonder.

A horseman drives forward
to the barricade
with his reins tight.

During these one or two moments
when seeing the Beloved is possible,
what is the work of our lives?

WILD DEER, MY FRIEND

✳ ✳✳ ✳

WHO TRAVELED WITH ME FOR YEARS,
HOW IS IT NOW WITH US
CROSSING THIS VAST PLAIN SEPARATELY?

WHERE WE'RE GOING HAS NOT CHANGED,
BUT WITHOUT EACH OTHER'S COMPANY
OUR JOURNEY GROWS FRIGHTENING.

I KEEP ASKING EVERYWHERE, "WHO
CAN TAKE THE WILD DEER'S PLACE? KHIDR?"
IS THAT GUIDE OF GUIDES APPROACHING?
I HEAR FOOTSTEPS.

BUT HE SEPARATED US BEFORE,
TURNING JOY TO GRIEF.
MAYBE HE WILL CHANGE IT BACK!

THIS TIME OF YEAR WHEN GOD
GIVES MANY GIFTS
THE LINE CAME TO ME
FROM THE QUR'AN
WHEN ZACHARIAH CRIES OUT,
*DON'T LEAVE ME
WITHOUT CHILDREN!*

✳ ✳✳ ✳

When Prophet Zachariah's wife Elizabeth was unable to
conceive, he cried out to the Lord, the Hearer of supplication,
with his plea. The son born to them was John the Baptist.

ONE DAY THERE WAS A RARE SPIRIT
SITTING BESIDE THE ROAD.

A TRAVELER WHO WAS DETERMINED TO REACH
THE GREAT SIMURGH BIRD WALKED BY.

"HAVE YOU BEEN GIVEN SOME SIGN
THAT SENDS YOU THIS WAY?
NO ONE HAS KNOWN, TILL NOW, WHICH WAY TO HEAD.

THE SUN PUT ITS   BAG OF FIRE IN ONE OF THE SCALE PANS.
WHAT HAVE   YOU FOUND TO BALANCE WITH THAT?"

THE TRAVELER   HAD NO ANSWER.

            WAS IT KHIDR   SITTING
            BESIDE THE   ROAD ASKING?

                    WAIT HERE
                    TILL HE COMES
                    AGAIN.

Sit by this spring and weep,
remembering those you've loved
that have died. Say your sadness
like a summer rain.
Merge into the river
made of such tribute.

Hold tight to the stem
of the rose you've been given,
learn what such a friend is worth.
Write that in the margin
and memorize it.

The strategy of this earth
Is to pull companions apart.
But what I write here
does not flow from anything material.

This poetry mixes soul with mind.
It's a seed held in music
As in warm ground.

The fragrance you take in, listening,
Comes from a peaceful presence, not
the wild deer who left me here alone!

BRINGING A MESSAGE FROM THE OTHER WORLD.
HE SAID, "GREAT FALCON, CAN'T YOU SEE,
YOU ARE A NOBLE BIRD OF VISION,
YOU DON'T BELONG HERE IN THIS WORLD OF PAIN AND VICE.
A NEST IN HEAVEN WAITS FOR YOU,
A PERCH TO SUIT YOUR LOFTY STATURE,
YOU WILL FIND IT HIGH ATOP THE TREE OF PARADISE.

OH, CAN'T YOU HEAR THE ROYAL FALCONER
WHISTLING FOR YOU?
THEY ARE CALLING YOU BACK TO PARADISE
FROM HERE BELOW. TELL ME WHY ARE YOU
SO RELUCTANT
TO RETURN THERE?
WHAT IS IT ABOUT THIS WORLD
THAT FASCINATES YOU SO?"

*This Knowledge is never grasped
by the intellect's noose;
Untie the noose and you will obtain it.*

God is
like
the bird
of paradise.
Do not try to
snare Him by
spreading the net
of your thoughts.
In that net you will
find nothing but mind.

29

You hide your face

IN THE LEAVES,
AND OUR EYES
FILL WITH ROSEWATER,
SLEEPY AS A NARCISSUS
OPENING.

YOU SLIP AWAY
IN THE GARDEN SEASONS.
THE PURPLE VIOLETS,
THE WHITE LILY,

THEY CHANGE
AND YOU HURRY OFF.

SURFACE BUBBLES
OPEN THEIR EYES, AND VANISH.
HOW DIFFERENT IS THIS WORLD
FROM THOSE BUBBLES?

YOUR WAY
WITH A BODY-CUP
IS TO DRAIN
ITS LOVE-WINE.

DO THAT
TO US!

Am I Not Your Lord?

With this question Hafiz draws on a famous Qur'anic passage in which God is addressing our souls before creation. "Am I not your Lord?" can be understood as a kind of preflight instruction that we receive before undertaking our earthly journey.

Our emphatic "Yes!" establishes the trust and determination needed to complete the whole journey and forms the affirmation of faith within each breath.

The same question appears again in the Bible when Father Abraham hears the voice of his Beloved. "Am I not your Lord?" serves as a wake-up call to the prophet, reminding him of his divine connection even as he's weighed down by worldly concerns. Abraham doesn't hesitate. His immediate response is, "Yes! Here I am!—*Hineni!*—At Your service." Fully present, mindful, ever awake to God's abiding love, Abraham is never far from intimate conversation with the Divine. From the very beginning, the blessed ones among us, like Abraham, have come to a state of communion with that ineffable mystery from which we all arise. They live in the place where the question and answer have become one.

Emerging from outside space and time, the sacred call is resonating still. It echoes in the many cries near and far of those who need our full presence and attention. Injustice, violence, prejudice, and the lurking threats of environmental collapse and nuclear annihilation can easily turn us away to apathy and despair. May we who love this planet and its inhabitants feel love's quickening spirit and run, like Abraham, toward this need with our own "Yes!" that we might bring love into action. This kind of love emerges from the greater heart and knows no borders. It is a limitless power and source, easily recognizable but forever deep and mysterious. Its profound ability to awaken, to heal, and to grant life is beyond measure. Powerful and supreme, it changes everything.

We can begin every day, every minute, by rising up to love. Then each of us, in our own way, finds guidance as we step into love's compassionate embrace.

— Jonathan Granoff

Near midnight, in disarray
you come asking,
"Is it still like this,
my love, when you're old?"
Who would refuse to answer?
The same was heard before
the creation of the universe,
"Am I not your Lord?"

Whatever's poured then
must be drunk.
It may be pure soul,
merely grape wine,
or some combination, but say
Yes, as I have many times,
as we all once did in unison
outside time and space.
Never regret that answer.

MOST PEOPLE
SEE YOUR EYES AND CALL FOR HELP.

BUT HAFIZ KNOWS
THAT THE WINE YOU OFFER

IS THE WINE IN THE QUR'AN
OF THE QUESTION,
AM I NOT YOUR LORD?
THAT YOU POURED
AS WE SAID *YES!*

Don't worry

ABOUT LIVELIHOOD OR PROPERTY.
BE A SUBSISTENCE FOR YOUR FRIENDS.
A SITAR STRING DRAWN TIGHT. A DRUM.

Be almost empty
AND THE DREG-DRINKERS
WILL GATHER
TO TASTE.

We travelers live in the guesthouse with two doors, and we must leave.

Who cares if your life goes on
underneath a big dome or a small one?

The waiting station of pleasure and delight
always includes suffering. In Pre-Eternity
our souls all bound
themselves to that tragedy.

Solomon's magnificence,
his horse of wind, his grasp
of bird language, the good man
got nothing from these;
all of them were blown
away in the wind.

Now, Hafiz, how can the tongue
hidden in your pen
ever give thanks enough for the way people
pass on your poems from hand to hand?

Send those who can
be hired to cry out
in the lover's market:

"Lost! A wild daughter has been lost,
wearing a thin crown of foam
and a dark red dress.

She's dangerous!
She'll steal your mind,
and yet whoever finds her
can have my soul for a reward.

From wherever the shameless blushing
grape of a girl has gone,
bring her back
to the home of Hafiz, the poet."

Lost, a wild daughter
has been lost!

Don't worry so much
about the rogues and rakes,
You high-minded puritans.
You know the sins of others
Will not appear written
on your foreheads anyway.

Whether I am good or bad
is not exactly
to the point.

Go ahead
and be who you are.
This world we live in Is a farm,
and each of us reaps
our own wheat.

Whether we are drunk
or sober,
each of us is heading
for the street
of the Friend.

The temple,
the synagogue,
The church,
and the mosque
are all houses of love.

42

Thousands of Muslims, Hindus, and Christians pay homage at the shrine of the Sufi mystic Mu'in ud-din Chishti in Ajmer, India. Born in Persia a century before Hafiz, Chishti's poetry of Divine Love was a precursor to Hafiz's beloved verse.

43

ELOVED, YOU HAVE DESTROYED MY HEART
WITH AN ARROW I CAN'T ENDURE
or dare to remove.

I AM THIS FIELD YOU'VE PLOWED
IN LONG EVEN ROWS
SOWN WITH THE NORTH WIND
FRAGRANCE OF APPLE BLOSSOMS
BIRDSONGS AND CHILDREN LAUGHING.

I AM MORE LIKE EARTH NOW
THAN EVER BEFORE,
SEEDS GROWING IN GRATITUDE.

YOUR SUN AND MOON GLANCE
HAS TEMPTED ME OUT OF MY ROBE AGAIN
INTO A UNION BEYOND ALL GRIEF IMAGES.

FALLING INTO YOUR CLEAR LIGHT
HAS PLANTED MAJESTY IN MY SHOES.

NOW HAFIZ KICKS UP STARDUST
WHEREVER HE GOES.

Don't ask me to describe
the taste of my poison.

At the end of years of wandering
I've chosen a Friend.
Don't ask who!
I weep in the doorway.

Last night I heard you saying
what cannot be said.
Now you motion to me. *Don't tell.*

The pain of being
   in my room alone is really
      what cannot be spoken.

         So, like Hafiz, I walk
            the love-road, aware in a way
               that has no name.

بجای اشک روان در کنار من باشی   من این مراد ببینم نخود که نیم شبی

If only in the middle of the night in place of these flowing tears
I had you in my embrace.

I EXPERIENCE THE PARCHED DESERT
OF SEPARATION
AS AN OCEAN OF WATER.
I HAVE GROWN SO MUCH IN LOVE
THAT I QUENCH MY THIRST
BY THIRST ITSELF!

O WHY DID I
CRAVE FOR YOU, GOD?
WHAT IS THIS BEING TOSSED
BACK AND FORTH
FROM THE OCEAN
TO THE SHORE?

I HAVE LEFT THE WORLD
FOR YOU,
BUT I CANNOT FIND YOU
ANYWHERE!

*O my friend,
from the cloud
of guidance,
send rain!*

There's a difference
between the water
of Khidr's spring,
hidden in
the land of night,
so difficult to reach,

And our water here,
which comes down
from that narrow gorge
in the mountains
to the north,

From where on the road
you first see Shiraz,
the pass called
Allahu Akbar.

Opening
into praise!

During Hafiz's era, medieval caravans trekked across the high desert plateau from Isfahan, south to Shiraz. Just before reaching their final destination, the path cut through a narrow mountain gorge before opening out onto a wide overlook with one of the most beautiful vistas in all of Persia. Weary travelers marveled at the lush garden city below them and *Allahu Akbar!* would rise from their hearts and tongues. Thus, the pass came to be known by this utterance of spontaneous praise and delight.

The breath of the holy musk

will drift toward us on the dawn wind once more;
everything will begin to move.
The decrepit old world will be young once more.

The Judas tree with its ruddy blossoms will offer
wine to the jasmine, and the eye of the narcissus
will turn its loving gaze on the red peony.

The nightingale who has endured a grievous
separation will fly now to the court of the rose,
demanding reparations with his wild cries.

If I've left the orthodox mosque and made my way
to the tavern of ruin, don't scold me. The preachers'
sermons are long-winded and the day is soon over.

Heart, listen to me; if you postpone the delight
of today until tomorrow, who will guarantee
that our cash in the bank will still be here in the morning?

Keep folding the cup during the month of Shaban*
    because this sun-cup will disappear from sight
        until the celebratory night at the end of Ramadan.

        The rose is a precious being; its intimate conversation
            is a gift from God. It has found its way to the garden
                through one gate, and will leave through the other.

            Musician, please listen!
                What we have here is a gathering
                    of friends, so sing songs and ghazals.

            Why keep jabbering
                about what has happened
                    and what may happen next?

*The month that precedes the fasting of Ramadan.

48

For your sake, Hafiz has come into the world.
As a way of saying farewell, come a step or two closer to him,
say good-bye, for he will be very soon gone.

Last night's storm
was a journey to the Beloved.
I surrender to that . . .
the wind that is my Friend,
and my work. Each night,
the lightning flashes,
every morning a breeze.
Not in some protected place,
but in the flood of the heart's pumping,
in the wind of a rosebud's opening out
that puts a small crown
on each narcissus.

A tired hand collapses,
exhausted,
that in the morning
holds your hair again.

Peace comes
when we are friends
together, remembering.

Hafiz! Your honest desire
and your benevolence
free the soul to emerge

as what it is.

We are the whirling ecstatics

WHO HAVE LET OUR HEARTS
GO TO THE WILD.
WE ARE MUSTY SCHOLARS OF LOVE,
AND OLD FRIENDS
OF THE CUP OF HEAVEN.

PEOPLE HAVE AIMED THE ARROW
OF GUILT A HUNDRED TIMES
IN OUR DIRECTION.
IT IS THROUGH YOU THAT
OUR WORK GOES ON AT ALL;
OH, TEACHER OF THE WAY, PLEASE
THROW US A GLANCE.
LET'S BE CLEAR ABOUT IT; WE HAVE
FALLEN OFF THE PATH.

Come, let's scatter roses

and pour wine in the glass;
we'll shatter heaven's roof
and lay a new foundation.
If sorrow raises armies to shed
the blood of lovers,
I'll join with the wine bearer
so we can overthrow them.
With a sweet string at hand
play a sweet song, my friend,
so we can clap and sing a song
and lose our heads in dancing.

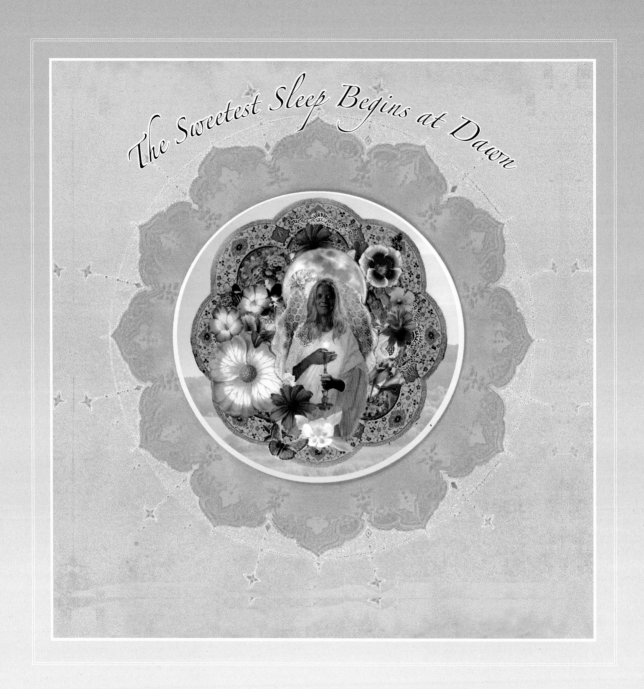

The Sweetest Sleep Begins at Dawn

BUT DON'T GIVE IN.
THIS CHANCE MAY NOT COME AGAIN!

YESTERDAY WE DIDN'T SEE EACH OTHER.
FOR ME, THERE'S NO PURPOSE
WITHOUT THOSE GLANCES.

HELPLESS HAFIZ! KEEP USING WORDS,
FOR ON THIS PLANET'S SURFACE

THE ONLY LIFE-FORMS LEFT
ARE THOSE THAT GROW
IN THE GARDEN OF THESE POEMS.

*Remember
the day we met*

THE TASTE OF THAT MOMENT IN THIS.
AS THE GRIEF-RIVER ALL AROUND CARRIES US AWAY,
RECALL A GARDEN WITH THE GARDENER
QUIETLY BENDING TO WORK.

ONE WHO HAD SECRETS WITH HAFIZ
THAT NO LONGER HAS TO KEEP THEM,
I REMEMBER THAT ONE NOW.

HAFIZ BROUGHT THE STORY OF YOUR RUBY LIP INTO HIS PEN.
NOW THE WATER OF ETERNAL LIFE FLOWS FROM IT.

آب حیوان می‌رود هر دم ز اقلامم هنوز   در قلم آورد حافظ قصهٔ لعل لبش

Hafiz: A Dazzling Turn

by Coleman Barks

For six centuries Hafiz has been scolded for inconsistency, for the giddy, slippery grace with which he skates from the profound to the comical to the passionate and then to a calm question, or almost anywhere. His poems have no apparent coherence, they scream down the ages. Many are unable to endure such authentic variety. Others find him a startling truth-teller and consummate poet. Goethe, for example, perhaps the most complex artist in the Western world, loved Hafiz. He saw in him a "twin."

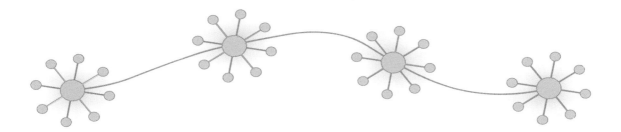

Hafiz is as elusive as the Beloved he adores, the presence that is everywhere and nowhere. The spiritual master Meher Baba (Hafiz was his favorite poet) said that "instead of the pearl inside Hafiz's poetry, most people see the oyster." The real meanings of Hafiz's poems, as one might expect, have been in great dispute, the sensual and spiritual being so hopelessly tangled. It is this equilibrium that gives the famous jewel-like effect. Delicate and tough, a crafted danger, full of wit as well as abandon, Hafiz's lyric is one of the rare mysteries of world literature.

With Hafiz the conventional divisions of awareness do not apply. Intellect, feeling, spiritual intuition, and the sensory grasp of moment and place all meld into a many-faceted, transparent whole. Hafiz is a shape-shifter, and each poem plays in the risk of soul-change. Hafiz moves along the edge that so many have longed to discover, where soul-body and language-music distinctions dissolve, and a new life form is born of their love.

Hafiz says, "How can you walk the true path, unless you step out of your own nature?" This is the paradox he embodied. His poems are entirely natural, and yet they've stepped over the boundary into a madness of surrender.

"O you, if you ever get lost enough to realize God, then you'll be dust at the feet of a Perfect Master."

Becoming particles is Hafiz's image of this happening. On the forehead of a man, on the doorsill, or suspended in water, the granule of matter doesn't care where it is. Hafiz's poetry has that grainy feel, particulate in line and image and yet unified in the overall powder of his joy. Hafiz says, "A Master cannot only turn dust to gold but dust into an alchemy that changes everything to gold."

Consider this metaphor for his poetry. The sound of rain is language being used. Silence is an orchard when it's not raining, the ground moisture being quietly drawn up into the fruit trees. Then there's the Hafiz-place, in between silence and speaking, when it's quit raining, but a rain-like dripping continues in the orchard. His poetry is a peace so fine it keeps overflowing, as though from nowhere.

WINE AND LOVE

I gave reason wine as a provision for the road
and sent him out of the city of existence.

نهاد م عقل را ره توشه ازمی   زشهرِ هستیش کردم روانه

The Sufi Master-poets often compare love with wine. Wine is the most fitting figure for love because both intoxicate. But while wine causes self-forgetfulness, love leads to Self-realization.

The behavior of the drunkard and the lover are similar; each disregards the world's standards of conduct and each is indifferent to the opinion of the world. But there are worlds of difference between the course and the goal of the two: the one leads to subterranean darkness and denial; the other gives wings to the soul for its flight to freedom.

The drunkenness of the drunkard begins with a glass of wine, which elates his spirit and loosens his affections and gives him a new view of life that promises a forgetfulness from his daily worries. He goes on from a glass to two glasses, to a bottle; from companionship to isolation, from forgetfulness to oblivion—oblivion, which in Reality, is the Original State of God, but which, with the drunkard, is an empty stupor—and he sleeps in a bed or a gutter. And he awakens in a dawn of futility, an object of disgust and ridicule to the world.

The lover's drunkenness begins with a drop of God's love, which makes him forget the world. The more he drinks the closer he draws to his Beloved, and the more unworthy he feels of the Beloved's love; and he longs to sacrifice his very life at his Beloved's feet. He, too, does not know whether he sleeps on a bed or in a gutter, and becomes an object of ridicule to the world; but he rests in bliss, and God the Beloved takes care of his body and neither the elements nor disease can touch it.

One out of many such lovers sees God face to face. His longing becomes infinite; he is like a fish thrown up on the beach, leaping and squirming to regain the ocean. He sees God everywhere and in everything, but he cannot find the gate of union. The Wine that he drinks turns into Fire in which he continuously burns in blissful agony. And the Fire eventually becomes the Ocean of Infinite Consciousness in which he drowns.

—Meher Baba

I am amazed, o rose, to see your kindness,
that you can sit together with the thorn—
you have apparently discovered
which way is useful in this time and place!

*The Garden is breathing
out the air
of Paradise today.*

Today. I can sense myself,
and this lively pure wine,
and this friend whose nature
approaches the divine.

It's all right if the beggar claims to be a king
today. His tent is a shadow thrown by a cloud;
his banqueting hall is a newly sown field.

Paradise is here in the simple tale that the May
meadow tells; the wise person lets the future
and its profits go, and accepts the cash now.

Please don't imagine that your enemy will ever
be faithful to you. The candle the hermit lights
will always flutter out in the worldly church.

Make your soul strong then
by letting it drink
the secret wine.
This rotten world has its own
plans to press our dust into bricks.

My life is a black book.
But don't rebuke a drinker
like me too much.
No human being can ever read
the words written
on his own forehead.

When Hafiz's coffin comes by,
it'll be all right to follow behind.

Although he is a captive of sin,
he is on his way
to the Garden.

راست چون سوسن و گل از اثر صحبت پاک   بر زبان بود مرا آنچه ترا در دل بود

I as the white lily
and you Beloved as the red rose,
we were in pure companionship.
And whatever was in your heart
was spoken by my tongue.

*A*LL I WANT IS TO BE NEAR YOU.
PRAISE GOD FOR THIS DESIRE,
AND LET IT INTENSIFY!

PRIESTS AND ELDERS HAVE A DIFFERENT VIEW.
 "DRUNKEN SOTS," THEY CALL US LOVERS.

 PEOPLE WITH NOTHING THAT THEY WANT,
 LET THEM LIVE THEIR DIM RIGHTEOUSNESS.

DARLING, MY SOUL, SEPARATED FROM YOU,
HAS NO WORDS BUT WEEPING.

THE CYPRESS TRIES TO HOLD YOUR GESTURES.
THE MOON, YOUR LOOK.

HAFIZ DOES NOT MUCH CARE ANYMORE
FOR EVENING DISCOURSE
OR MORNING PRAYER,

WHEN THERE'S SOME SMALL CHANCE
YOU'LL LEAN DOWN TO KISS.

Loving you this way is driving me mad,
for already
I talk to the moon and see angels in my sleep.

I have the treasure
in my sleeve
but my purse
is empty.
I have
the world-revealing cup
and I am
the dust
of the road.

ONE ROSY FACE
FROM THE WORLD'S
GARDEN

FOR US
IS ENOUGH

AND THE SHADE
OF THAT ONE CYPRESS
IN THE FIELD
STROLLING ALONG GRACEFULLY

FOR US IS ENOUGH.

I WANT TO BE FAR AWAY FROM PEOPLE WHOSE WORDS
AND DEEDS DON'T MATCH. AMONG THE MOROSE AND HEAVY-
HEARTED, A HEAVY GLASS OF WINE
FOR US IS ENOUGH.

SOME PEOPLE SAY THAT GOOD DEEDS WILL EARN THEM
A GATED HOUSE IN HEAVEN. BEING RAKES AND NATURAL BEGGARS,
A ROOM IN THE TAVERN
FOR US IS ENOUGH.

SIT DOWN BESIDE THE STREAM SOMETIME AND WATCH
LIFE FLOW PAST. THAT BRIEF HINT OF THIS WORLD
THAT PASSES BY SO SWIFTLY
FOR US IS ENOUGH.

LOOK AT THE FLOW OF MONEY AND THE SUFFERING
OF THE WORLD. IF THIS GLIMPSE OF PROFIT AND LOSS
IS NOT ENOUGH
FOR YOU, FOR US IT IS ENOUGH.

THE DEAREST COMPANION OF ALL IS HERE. WHAT
ELSE IS THERE TO LOOK FOR? THE DELIGHT OF A FEW WORDS
WITH THE SOUL FRIEND
FOR US IS ENOUGH.

DON'T SEND ME AWAY FROM YOUR DOOR, OH, GOD,
EVEN TO PARADISE. YOUR ALLEYWAY, COMPARED
TO ALL SPACE AND TIME,
FOR US IS ENOUGH.

IT'S INAPPROPRIATE, HAFIZ, FOR YOU TO COMPLAIN
OF YOUR GIFTS FROM FATE. YOUR NATURE IS LIKE WATER;
YOUR BEAUTIFULLY FLOWING POEMS
FOR US ARE ENOUGH.

I followed the path

of the mad libertines
long enough, until I was able,
with the consent
of intelligence,
to put my greediness into prison.

I didn't find the way to the nest
of the great bird of the far
mountain by myself.
I made the trip with the help
of the bird of Solomon.

Seek satisfaction in what comes
contrary to your habit.
I found interior concentration
At last in your disheveled
head of hair.

Bring a cooling shade
over my interior burning,
you are a hidden treasure—
because it is out of the melancholy
of desire for you
that I have wrecked this house.

I repented and swore
that I would never kiss
the salty lip of the cup bearer again;
but now I am biting
my own lip, and I wonder
why I ever listened to an idiot.

Being a model of modesty
or drunkenness
is not up to us. Whatever the Master
of Pre-Eternity told me to do, I did.

Because of this grace,
I have a longing
for the Garden of Paradise,
even though I spent
long years as a doorkeeper
in the tavern.

Here at the door of old age,
the fact that the companionship
of Joseph has graced me
is a reward for my patience
when living like Jacob
in his house of sorrow.

No reciter of scripture
who stands
in the prayer niche
of the Firmament
has ever enjoyed
such delight
as I have received
from the wealth of the Qur'an.

Ask any physician and he'll tell you there is no cure for my pain.
Without the Beloved, I am heartbroken, sick. With him, I'm well. It's as simple as that.
Even though He says, "Don't bring your load of troubles into this Street,"
I will never leave the place in which the Beloved dwells.

*B*efitting a fortunate slave,
carry out every command of the Master,
without any question of why and what.

About what you hear from the Master, never say it is wrong, because,
my dear, the fault lies in your own incapacity to understand him.

I am the slave of the Master who has released me from ignorance;
whatever my Master does is of the highest benefit to all concerned.

*W*ash your hands of this coppery existence
so that one day you will get the alchemy of love and become gold.

*T*he lover says to the Master . . .

You have taught me something
that has made me forget everything.
You have created in me a desire that says do not desire anything.

You have given me that *One Word* which says: words mean nothing.
O Master, I was seeking God and thought Him this and that.

Now, you have given me something of which even
my imagination cannot produce its shadow.

بکام تا نرساند مرا لبش جو نای

نصیحت همه عالم بگوش من باد ست

UNTIL HE TAKES ME
TO HIS LIPS LIKE A REED,
ALL THE ADVICE
OF THE WORLD PASSES
BY MY EAR LIKE THE WIND.

How marvelous the music
of that musician is who calls up love.
The tunes he strikes up in different modes
all go to a different place.

I hope the world will never
be deprived of the cries
of lovers. When they cry out, their
harmonies stretch us out into eternity.

The beautiful bride of the world
approaches, but not to marry anyone!

Watch. One bride leaves
as another comes.

The cypress, the tulip,
a line of gowns.

We are beggars here,
but don't ask what we're begging for!
Whatever it is shows in our faces.

So I said to tease the beauty, "My moon,
if we kissed, could I endure the love?"

"Hafiz," she laughed, *"kiss on!
Your lips won't stain the moon."*

*The rosebush
of your beauty
did not bloom by itself.
It blossomed
from the breath
of the spirit of our hearts.*

گلبن حشت نه خود شد دلفروز
مادم همت برو بگماشتیم

*D*ear friends, there's a Friend
inside the night. *Remember.*

And the duty of serving others,
remember that.

In the middle of any excitement,
when the musical moan
of your lover comes, *remember.*

As you put your hopeful hand on her waist,
as the face of one bringing you a song
lights with recognition,
remember.

Just as your horse
is passing the others,
remember.

As you sit down to
take command,
remember Hafiz's face,
and the way of kindness.

As the empty
threshold does,

Remember.

*H*oard each joyous moment that comes to you.
No one knows how it all will end.

در شبِ تار رستیم نبوس است

O

SUCH A

DELICATE PEARL

HOW I LONG

TO PIERCE IT

IN THE

DARKEST

NIGHT.

In the Beginningless Beginning, the Sufis say we were given the treasure of the precious pearl of wisdom. Its essence is a pure drop of rain that falls from heaven onto the ocean of light within the heart, then sinks and falls into the shell made of unshakeable faith in the Holy One.

وه که در دانهٔ حسین نازک

GOD,
OF WHAT IS THE MIRROR
OF YOUR BEAUTY MADE
THAT MY SIGHS
HAVE NO POWER
TO LEAVE ANY TRACE
UPON IT?

یارب این آئینهٔ حسن چه جوهر دارد

که در و آه مرا قوّت تأثیر نبود

The Light accepts this pure drop and takes it deep inside. There it matures into a luminous pearl resplending like a full moon in the darkest night. The joyful, radiant heart then becomes the loving place where truth dwells and all lives turn in prayer.

BRING NEWS OF OUR UNION
AND MY SOUL WILL RISE UP!
IN LOVE, I'LL RISE UP.
FROM THE SNARES OF EXISTENCE,
I'LL RISE TO YOU.
I AM THE BIRD OF HEAVEN.

ON'T ALLOW

YOUR INWARD BEING

TO BE HURT

BY WHAT YOU HAVE

OR HAVE NOT.

BE GLAD

BECAUSE

EVERY PERFECT THING

IS ON ITS WAY

TO NONEXISTENCE.

With the burst of one ray of splendor

THE BEAUTY OF YOUR FACE
REFLECTS ALL OF THESE FORMS
IN THE MIRROR OF IMAGINATION.

Like Jesus, ascend

ON THE NIGHT OF YOUR DEATH
STRAIGHT UP TO HEAVEN

SO THAT FROM YOUR LANTERN
A HUNDRED RAYS OF LIGHT
WILL REACH THE SUN.

*From your lovers on this path, the breeze has learned
how to rend the black garments of night
at the moment of dawn.*

Come so I may draw up

بیا که لعل و گهر در نثار مقدم تو
ز گنج خانهٔ دل می‌کشم بخزن چشم

rubies and pearls from the treasure of my heart
to the treasury of my eye and shower them before your footstep.

When the One whom I love

ACCEPTS THE WINE,
THEN THE SHOP OF FALSE IDOLS COLLAPSES.
I HAVE DROPPED IN A HEAP
ON THE EARTH, CRYING,
IN THE HOPE THAT I WILL FEEL
A TOUCH OF HIS HAND.

I HAVE FALLEN
LIKE A FISH INTO DEEP WATER
IN THE HOPE THAT THE FRIEND
WILL CATCH ME IN HIS NET.

*Do as much as you can while you walk the earth,
for under the earth time holds many who can do nothing.*

It is the Night of Power

THIS NIGHT OF POWER IS BETTER THAN A THOUSAND MONTHS.
THE ANGELS DESCEND WITH EVERY DECREE
BY THEIR LORD'S PERMISSION.
PEACE! ALL THROUGH THE BLESSED NIGHT
UNTIL THE RISE OF DAWN!

The Qur'an

LAST NIGHT
AS DAWN WAS BREAKING
HE GAVE ME SALVATION FROM SORROW
AND IN THAT DARKEST NIGHT
HE GAVE ME THE WATER OF ETERNAL LIFE.

If everyone in the world
advised against my loving you,
still I would.

One lives in the zikr circle
so that the round knot
in the Beloved's hair
will be undone.

*Both the happinesses and the sorrows
of the world will pass away.
So it is better to remain
peaceful throughout.*

The Sufis call *zikr* the breath of gratitude, the remembrance of God breathing us and everything into existence. Compassion and love open a door to this reality. With each out-breath, we let go of that which separates us from others. With each in-breath, we affirm the presence of the Sacred. This luminous breath, empty of self and filled with love, has the power to dispel all darkness.

You that drain the sky's clear cup,

WANDERERS OF THE IMAGINATION
TAKE A THOUSAND YEARS
TO CLIMB THE PATH TO YOU.

YOU ARE THE EYE AND THE LAMP WE USE.
THE SUN AND THE MOON?
JUST THE SIMPLEST BITS
LEFT ON THE EDGE OF YOUR TRAY.

PRAISING YOU GAVE MY MIND A DAUGHTER
THAT NOW I BRING YOU FOR A BRIDE.

THIS POEM BE WITNESS
I SERVE YOUR KINDNESS
LIKE A SLAVE.

unless you step out of the boundary of your own nature?
You must leave the abode of your nature, temperament, and thoughts,
Unless you do so, you cannot reach the lane of Truth!

God's Light!

I see where and what that is,
But who drinks the dregs in this wine-house?
I see the door, and the prayer rug
pointing its need, and the archway.

I see who leads the way to Mecca.
I see the dignity of being a lover,
and the disgrace, and the playfulness.
I see the Kaaba.

I catch an eastwind fragrance every morning.
I see the point of unity in all creation,
with no why or how.
I see poor philosophy so far from reality.

I see that my fancy images fail.
But to whom shall I say what's left?
Don't come complaining that Hafiz keeps claiming
"I see, I see," him and his crowd of God-lovers!

WHEN YOUR IMAGE PASSES
BEFORE THE ROSE GARDEN OF THE EYE,
THE HEART COMES TO THE WINDOW OF SIGHT.

THE LOVER AND THE BELOVED

God is love. And Love must love. And to love there must be a Beloved. But since God is Existence, infinite and eternal, there is no one for Him to love but Himself. And in order to love Himself He must imagine Himself as the Beloved—whom He as the Lover imagines He loves.

Beloved and Lover implies separation. And separation creates longing; and longing causes search. And the wider and the more intense the search the greater the separation and the more terrible the longing. When longing is most intense separation is complete, and the purpose of separation, which was that Love might experience itself as Lover and Beloved, is fulfilled; and union follows.

And when union is attained, the Lover knows that he himself was all along the Beloved whom he loved and desired union with; and that all the impossible situations that he overcame were obstacles which he himself had placed in the path to himself. To attain union is so impossibly difficult because it is impossible to become what you already are! Union is nothing other than knowledge of oneself as the Only One.

— Meher Baba

BY LOVING,
YOUR WHOLE BEING WILL BE CHANGED
AND YOUR LIFE WILL END IN FREEDOM.

Both human beings & spirits

Painting by Laurie Blum

take their sustenance from the existence of Love.
The practice of devotion is a good way to arrive
at happiness in both worlds.

Hafiz's tomb shrine in his beloved Shiraz lies among the roses of the Musalla Gardens on the banks of the Ruknabad.
A place of pilgrimage for centuries, the tomb and surrounds are treated with great reverence. Visitors consult
Hafiz's *Divan* for divine guidance, as do hundreds of thousands of people in Persia, India, and around the world.

Bring all
the wine
that's left!

When we're dead
and wandering Paradise,
we won't find a place
more beautiful
than this stream
called Ruknabad,
by the gardens
with their roses
in the town of Shiraz.

THE GREAT LOVERS

HAVE FOUND   THEIR WAY
INTO THE   DEEP OCEAN,
AND DROWNED   WITHOUT EVER TAKING

ONE DROP FROM THE SEA.

My moon went out of town yesterday
and it seemed to me like a year.

We have turned the face

of our dawn studies

toward the ecstatic's way.

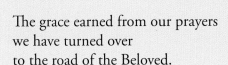

The grace earned from our prayers
we have turned over
to the road of the Beloved.

The hot brand which we have pressed
onto our lunatic hearts
is so intense it would set fire
to the straw piles of a hundred
reasonable ascetics.

The Sultan of Pre-Eternity
gave us a casket of Love's grief
as a gift; therefore we have turned
our face toward this wrecked
caravanserai that we call "the world."

From now on I will leave
no doors in my heart open
for the love of beautiful creatures.

I have placed
the signet seal of Her lips
on the door of this house.
It's time to turn away
from make-believe under our robes

patched so many times.
The foundation for our work
is a tricksterish attitude
that sees through
all these games.

How can this wobbly old ship
keep going when in the end
we have set for our soul
the task of finding the pearl
on the ocean floor?

The man next door,
whom I have called a parasite
of reason and an intellectual
is—thanks to God—like us,
actually faithless
and without heart.

We are content, just as Hafiz is,
with a phantom of you.
Oh, God, how pitifully poor
our aspirations are,
And how estranged and distant,
how far we are from union!

There is this matter

of the light in my eyes.

If you want to know the Friend,
don't expect elegant arguments!

Demand a blessing …

 from one who gives you joy.

Happy is the wind that rises in the garden of beauty.

And then He gave me
a goblet of wine
whose luminance
burst through the heavens
bringing Venus to dance
and the lutists to sing,
"Drink!"

Like the candle of morning
my life will disappear
when it's illumined by the Sun of Your compassion.

No need for a candle in this gathering

In our soiree the beautiful face
of my darling is a full moon.

No need for perfume
in our banquet.
The only fragrance I need
is the musk of your tresses.
No need for sugar here
sweetness of your lips suffices.

In our religion wine is permitted
but tonight it'd be forbidden
without your beautiful face.

My ears? Tied to the sound of the flute
and the strumming of the harp.
My eyes? Caught up in your ruby lips
and the sharing of this goblet.

Don't talk with me of shame.
I've become infamous from this "shame."
Why do you speak with me of my name?

I'm ashamed of whatever name I used to have.
We are: Drunk, head-whirling, rogue
love glance playing.

Who in this whole town isn't like us, like this?
Hafiz, don't sit for a moment without wine
and a beloved for the ages.

These are the days for roses and jasmines.

Holy Days.

Wherever You Turn

There is the Face of God

Even if the two worlds are uprooted and destroyed,
the light of my eyes will stay fixed on the road
of the Friend's expected arrival.

گر باد فتنه هر دو جهان را بهم زند   ما و چراغ چشم و ره انتظار دوست

The glory of being young
HAS COME AGAIN!
THE LIGHT WIND, THE BASIL.

THE CHILD THAT LOOKS SO WISE
IS RUNNING STRAIGHT
TO YOU FOR A KISS!

THE MOON IS A POLO BALL,
AND ALSO A POLO STICK!

BE HELPFUL ON THE SURVIVAL ARK,
EVEN THOUGH SAFETY
IS NOT THE POINT.

EVERY GUEST DIES IN THE END.
BUT FOR NOW,
JOSEPH HAS BEEN RELEASED FROM PRISON!

LIFT YOUR WINE IN SALUTE TO FREEDOM.
DON'T BE TRAPPED, AS OTHERS HAVE,
BY SOME QUOTE FROM THE QUR'AN.

ABANDON, SAYS THE ROSE,
AND NIGHTINGALES BEGIN.

Seawater seemed a bargain to cross

when your offer came.

THEN A STORM BLEW IN,
AND THE RATIO CHANGED
BETWEEN THE INDIAN OCEAN
AND ITS PEARLS!

THE PEARL THAT WAS NEVER
INSIDE THE SHELL OF SPACE AND TIME,
WE ASKED FOR THAT FROM PEOPLE
LOST AT THE OCEAN'S EDGE.

*HAFIZ, PERHAPS IN PURSUIT OF THE PEARL OF UNION
YOU WILL FORM AN OCEAN FROM YOUR TEARS
AND DROWN IN IT.

FOR MANY YEARS MY HEART WANTED
SOMETHING FROM ME,
NOT KNOWING THAT IT WAS ITSELF IT WANTED:

THE DESIRE FOR JAMSHID'S CUP,
WHEREIN ALL EXISTENCE CAN BE SEEN,
EXCEPT FOR THE CHALICE ITSELF, THAT IS.

THERE WAS A MAN BELOVED OF GOD
WHO CRIED OUT TO GOD, "WHY
HAVE YOU FORSAKEN ME?"

I TOOK THE RIDDLE INTO A TAVERN
AND ASKED THE ONE WHO SERVED.

HE SAID, "SOME SECRETS MUST BE KEPT,
NOT TOLD TO THE WORLD AT LARGE.
THE ROSEBUD AND THE SOUL
WRITE MYSTERIES ON THEIR MARGINS
FOLD WITHIN FOLD. STAY CLOSED AND WAIT."

"YOUR WINEGLASS IS THE ALL-REVEALING CUP"
"GIVEN BEFORE CREATION!"

When King Jamshid looked into the goblet of wine in
his heart and saw his own image perfectly reflected, he
experienced the moment of union, God-realization.

SEE THE SPEED
OF POETRY
TRAVERSING
SPACE AND TIME

FOR THIS CHILD
OF ONE NIGHT
IS TRAVELING
THE ROAD
OF ONE YEAR.

طی مکان ببین و زمان در سلوک شعر

کاین طفل یکشبه ره صد ساله می رود

عاقبت منزل ما وادی خاموشیست
حالیا غلغله در گنبد افلاک انداز

*I*n the end
our abode
will be the valley
of the silent ones.

For now
let us raise a riot
in the dome
of the highest heaven.

Come!
For the foundations
of the palace of desire
are weak.

Bring wine!
For the footings
of life
are on the wind.

If you feel weak, feeble,
and powerless, well,
so does the breeze.

Being sick on the Path
is a hundred times better
than a healthy mind
in a healthy body.

If you would
like to fill
the world
with beauty
eternally

ask the
morning breeze
to lift for a moment
the veil
from your face.

بیا که قصر امل سخت سست بنیادست

بیار باده که بنیاد عمر بر بادست

O nightingale of the morning

REJOICE! FOR YOUR HEART
HAS BECOME UNITED
WITH THE ROSE
AND ALL OF THE LOVE-SONGS
IN THE MEADOW
ARE NOW YOURS.

◆ ◆ ◆ ◆

دلت بوصل گل ای بلبل صبا خوش باد   که در چمن همه گلبانگ عاشقانه تست

The morning breeze comes back,
and from the southern desert
the lapwing returns.

The dove's soft song about roses,
I hear that again.

The tulip, who understands
what the lily says,
went away, but now she's back.

With the sound of a bell,
strength and gentleness.

Hafiz broke his vow
and damaged his heart,

but now, for no reason,
his Friend forgives that, and turns,
and walks back up to his door.

A GATHERING OF GOOD FRIENDS

Talking quietly outdoors.
The infinite mystery
of all this love.

If someone doesn't want the pleasure
Of such an openhearted garden,

Companionship, no life itself
Must be against his rules!

I will give you my heart

containing the pearl
of the secret of beauty and love
if you treat it kindly.

In the school of God and in the company of the Perfect Master,
try, try, and try again so that one day you also become perfect.

Wash your hands of books if you are my classmate,
because the lesson of Love is in no book.

⁓⟨✦⟩⁓

By the light of a sheikh a pilgrim finds the Beloved.
Heart-lost, at life's end, help us taste that wine!
The time of judging who's drunk and who's sober,
who's right or wrong, who's closer to God
or farther away, all that's over!

This caravan is led instead by a great delight,
the simple joy that sits with us.
That is the grace.
Hafiz! It may be that you've just poured the toast
that will wash love free of all its pictures.

*G*o by yourself!
For the gates of righteousness are narrow.
Take hold of the wine cup for nothing can equal
the dearness of life.

I've heard nothing lovelier

than the melody of love
a keepsake lingering in this whirling azure dome.

Dear God, place light in my heart, light in my tongue, light in my hearing, light in my sight, light behind me, light in front of me, light on my right, light on my left, light above me and light below me; place light in my sinew, in my flesh, in my blood, in my hair, and in my skin; place light in my soul and make light abundant for me; make me light and grant me light.

A prayer attributed to the Holy Prophet, may Love surround him.

O soul at peace!

Return to your Lord
well pleased and well-pleasing
enter with my servants into the garden

The Qur'an

*The Journey to Light reaches its ultimate fulfillment
when the clarity of pure wisdom
realizes the Great Mystery
of God's Infinite Love resonating in the human heart.*

HAFIZ
AND THE
WELLSPRING
OF
CREATIVITY

A BIOGRAPHY
BY PETER BOOTH

Khwāja Shams-ud-Dīn Muhammad Hāfez-e Shīrāzī, known by his pen name Hafiz, meaning "one who has memorized the Qur'an," was born in Shiraz, Iran, in the early fourteenth century CE. Despite being born in this provincial corner of the world and despite the passage of more than six hundred years, he is still, without doubt, not only Iran's most popular poet but also the most influential writer to ever take up a pen. Indeed, Hafiz's verses are a wellspring of poetic archetypes, and these have flooded the great traditions of Persia, Central Asia, and beyond, with his lyrics being sung from the shores of the Euphrates, in what is present-day Turkey, to the heights of India's Deccan Plateau. Even today the vocabulary of love in these regions has a strong mystical flavor derived from his revelatory writings.

Hafiz's artistry poured over into the West as well, where generations of writers hungry for a poetic vocabulary containing the mysteries of existence devoured his work. Hafiz significantly influenced innumerable writers and artists, including Goethe, Thoreau, Brahms, Dickinson, Lorca, Nietzsche, Byron, Pushkin, and Emerson—who referred to him as "a poet's poet" and "such is the only man I wish to see and be." It was Emerson who crafted numerous translations of Hafiz into English from German translations, after reading Goethe's *West-Eastern Divan*. It is also believed that Emerson, while under the influence of Hafiz's writings, created his finest poem, "Bacchus," which, according to the literary critic Harold Bloom, set the dialectic of American poetry.

"The only man I wish to see and be."
—Ralph Waldo Emerson

This opened the floodgates allowing Hafiz's conceptions and imagery to flow into the mainstream of American literature and art, where they are still visible to this day. Similar phenomena occurred in England, Germany, France, Spain, and Russia. In our time as well, a new generation is in search of the mysteries of spiritual unfoldment revealed in the writings of this incomparable genius.

As a figure from antiquity, little is known about Hafiz's life and personality. For this we must turn to his poetry, and the voice we find here has resonated through the centuries. But first, let's briefly set the stage in fourteenth-century Iran, then take a look at two major events early in Hafiz's life—an encounter with a romantic beauty that led to an encounter with a Divine Beauty. Both inspired the sublime poetry that followed.

Fourteenth-century Shiraz was known as the city of poets, saints, gardens, wine, nightingales, and philosophers. Heralded as the Athens of Iran, its natural beauty and royal patronage attracted the great minds and talents of the age. In poetry, the art form Shiraz is best known for, a gradual transformation spanning several centuries, had resulted in verse that supported mystical transformation. These poets—Rumi, Saadi, Farid al-Din Attar, and others—were now revealing the mysteries of love between man and God. Despite this great development, however, the full poetic, multifaceted power of the Persian language had not yet been achieved. This task was left to an unattractive, unassuming young man of humble birth whose inner pearl of poetic speech was about to be revealed.

To place Hafiz's lifetime in some perspective, he lived less than a century after the death of Saint Francis of Assisi and about fifty years after the death of Rumi; he was a contemporary of Chaucer, and was born near the end of Dante's life. Most accounts speak of his family as being either in the bakery or coal business. One day, while making deliveries for the family business, Hafiz sighted an aristocratic beauty standing on a balcony and fell completely in love with her. Well aware that, given their differences in social status, there was no way he could gain her hand—and anyway she was as elegant and beautiful as he was squat and ugly—Hafiz resolved to obtain her through spiritual means. This meant completing the severe great trial of the *chilla-nashini*. Practiced not just in Iran but throughout the East, this trial, rooted in ancient Hebrew tradition and undertaken by Christ in the Judean Desert, required the practitioner to stay within a circle for forty days and nights without eating or sleeping. If successful, the desired boon was granted.

So great was Hafiz's love for Shakh-i-Nabat —"branch of sugar cane"— as she was named, he succeeded. On the fortieth night the archangel Gabriel appeared and asked Hafiz his desire. Overwhelmed by Gabriel's radiance, and the penetrating impact of his speech, Hafiz forgot completely about the mere branch of sugarcane and asked instead for God. For if the beauty of Gabriel, being only His messenger, was this resplendent, how much more beautiful must God be?

Gabriel directed Hafiz to the God-realized Master,* Mohammad Attar, thus launching him on his journey of self-realization. Still under the reverberating effects of Gabriel's speech, Hafiz began writing poetry. It was these attempts to capture the power of Gabriel's sublime words that led him to transform the Persian ghazal.

✳ ✳

* See glossary for "God-realization" and related terms.

And whereas others before him—Jalal al-Din Rumi being the best known—wrote poetic narratives about the intoxication of being in the company of divine beings, Hafiz created a form that actually produced this intoxication. In short, he crafted a poetic form of spiritual revelation.

Hafiz tells us that Gabriel's speech was sharply piercing—shot with great precision into his heart. To try to capture this divine language, Hafiz gave a revolutionary overhaul to the ghazal, removing any progression between couplets, instead crafting each couplet as an arrow that appears suddenly and dramatically, as if from nowhere, unique in its power and beauty—its power coming from its beauty—essentially a lightning bolt of revelation shattering the foundations of the hearer's separateness from God.

Any sense of progression in the ghazal is accompanied by the anticipation of the next couplet's arrival, but this expectation detracts from the sudden wonder of each couplet's appearance. By the end of any ghazal the reader's presumption of *what is* has been uprooted or shattered; one's heart becomes captivated, enthralled, overwhelmed with intoxication, and often left in significant pain from separation and longing. In some of today's Sufi orders in Iran it is forbidden for novitiates to read Hafiz, this piercing style being known for driving people mad and even knocking very learned men unconscious. This shattering of the foundation of the reader's limited perception of reality was, for Hafiz, a primary element of spiritual unfoldment, as the upheaval of each foundation brings the lover closer to Union with the Beloved. These states are clearly defined within Sufism and other mystical systems. Meher Baba said of Hafiz, however, "Yet there are very few

In short, he crafted a poetic form of spiritual revelation.

who understand the spiritual secrets which are revealed in his poetry. In fact, Khwaja (the Master) Hafiz has clearly narrated, one by one, all the stages of spirituality in his *Divan.* Every complete ghazal refers to a certain spiritual state and stage for one who can understand it."**

On this spiritual journey to Union with the limitless source of being, one's ego must cross the vast desert of separation. Hafiz knew that this is a journey in consciousness only, for as God is everywhere, there is no place to go. At journey's end the illusion of the limited self is removed and God comes face to face with Himself in a new eternal form. It is a sojourn not unlike making and breaking camps on the climb to Everest. Over the forty long years of his journey under Attar's guidance, Hafiz wrote a travelogue of each encampment and left a campfire burning for us there.

He also, after completing the journey, placed himself at the wellspring where the infinity of God's existence surges into the manifest realms of illusion. Here he took the clear and pure effulgence of Existence and passed it through archetypal prisms of exquisite poetic beauty, much as wavelengths of light reflect the scattering of particles and cloud patterns to give spectacular color to the rising and setting sun. This ability earned him the appellation of *Lisan al-ghayb,* or "the tongue of the hidden mysteries"; that is, one who possesses the gift to reveal the imperceptible—essentially the one who is the tongue of God.

Concurrent with and preceding Hafiz's journey was a gradual removal in Persian poetry of the conception of human sin and a vengeful, punishing God, and, in its place, the creation of a God of limitless love and compassion. This transformation began with Rabia of Basra and developed under Abu Sa'id Abul-Khayr, Farid al-Din Attar (who penned *The Conference of the Birds*), Ibn 'Arabi, and others, before finding its full flowering under Rumi. As Hafiz was a *gohar shanas,* a discerner of gems in the poetry of others (as was Emerson in our times), he borrowed liberally from these writers and brought these elements of unconditional love into his poetry. Part of the work of the tongue of the hidden, then, was to personify God as the Divine Beloved endowed with limitless love and compassion.

For this it was essential that the very limited and false concepts of original sin and salvation, pounded into human consciousness by religion down through the ages, be removed, and, in their place, an entirely new cosmology called *Irfan-e-esqheyani,* or the mysticism of Divine Love, be formed. Rumi and Hafiz were the main architects of this new cosmology, asserting that man's existence was not the result of original sin, but rather as the result of God's need to express His true nature as limitless, unconditional love. For this He needs someone other than Himself to love. To form this lover, God has to create a false separation—an "other," as it were. In the ensuing play between lover and Beloved and the growing experience of God as Infinite Love, there is no room for sin and damnation, as in reality neither exist. Simply, creation and man are brought about not out of sin, but out of Love.

❋ ❋

** Lord Meher, p. 860, online edition, accessed January 31, 2019.

The priests, mullahs, even most of the Sufi sheikhs were not about to accept this new view of creation and the entirely personal and private lover-Beloved relationship it allows for, as it puts them out of work; rather they continued their threats of damnation and insisted that salvation is possible only through their intercession. Hafiz railed against these hypocrites, seeing them as noxious weeds intent on strangling the rose, and as noisy crows drowning out the ecstatic melodies of the nightingale—destroying the garden's beauty and innocence. Accordingly, Hafiz took great care to see that every thread he stitched into his poetry was free not just of the conception of sin and salvation, but also of the equally limiting conceptions of morality:

> Do what you like but don't
> intentionally hurt anyone,
> in our religion this is the only sin.

Indeed, in keeping with the revelations of Saint Francis (who was also God-realized), and as a message to us in this age of extreme intellectualism, it is now the ecstatic beauty of the garden of nature piercing the veils of material consciousness that generates the supreme intelligence of higher consciousness and not the pages of learning. Additionally, it is the poetry that expresses this beauty that becomes the alchemy of the transformation of consciousness. Or, to put things in a Western context, rather than Jung's theory of archetypes forming a collective unconsciousness, with Hafiz it his construction of poetic archetypes that builds the highway from consciousness to superconsciousness. This is what he is up to.

To Hafiz, our very existence is the treasure of God's limitless Love. Accordingly, Hafiz assures us that it is perfectly alright for us to be ourselves, as each person is a unique pearl never to be duplicated. We do not have to conform to any models or conceptions of spirituality to be the true spiritual being that we already are.

Although Hafiz brings a number of revolutionary elements into the ghazal form, he, at the same time, leaves many of the old images and concepts intact so that his writing is familiar to the audience of his day. Then, within these old structures, the nightingale suddenly sings in registers never before heard; the poet pours a wine

. . . for this great, thrilling, and final journey of the soul, Hafiz's poetry is the perfect guide.

of an untasted vintage into the age-old goblet of the ghazal form. The pearl must have the shell to reach perfection; without the shell there is nothing, just the Ocean. Writing and singing within the accepted forms allows Hafiz's poetry to touch and then expand his audiences' experience of beauty and enthrall all at every level, even the uneducated.

The journey in Hafiz is best seen as a passage from the futility of trying to obtain the beauty by possessing the form, to moving away from form toward the experience of—and eventual union with—the limitless formless beauty existing in every form. As such, this journey is one into deeper and deeper ecstatic experiences. In this great expansion, morality has no place, as any moral structure involves rejection and acceptance which is always under the sway of those who place themselves as the high priests of any dichotomy. As they are judgmental, moral structures can have little or nothing to do with ecstasy and Divine Love. Accordingly, religion and morality are nowhere extolled in Hafiz's poetry, and in fact he rails against both.

Many believe that Hafiz wrote in a language of dual meaning, equally supporting at one and the same time a worldly love and a Divine Love; and that when he wrote about wine, lovers, and song, he wrote about getting drunk, making love, and singing ditties of carpe diem in the tavern, while at the same time using a highly crafted metaphorical language to reveal the deepest mysteries and divine beauty of God. It is, many suggest, his ability to do both, equally, that is the major hallmark of his genius. However, when we consider that Hafiz says the material world is an illusion that does not exist—the shell, as it were, whose only purpose is to produce the pearl of a unique eternal existence; and when we consider that his body of work is a travelogue describing the journey from the limited material experience of beauty to the far greater beauty of the Beloved, then we know this reading misses the essence of his poetry. Simply, you cannot stay drunk making love and enthralled with the beauty of the base camp while at the same time trying to scale the summit. Sooner or later one has to pack up and get on with it. And for this great, thrilling, and final journey of the soul, Hafiz's poetry is the perfect guide.

So suspend, if you will for a moment, your sense of disbelief at happenings way beyond our ken—the appearance of the archangel Gabriel, spiritual guidance at the hands of a God-realized Master, a poet inspired by Gabriel's voice, writing new archetypes on his way to God-realization. If you refute the possibility of these miraculous events then you will be hard-pressed, I believe, to account for the incomparable influence this poet has had on world literature, music, and art. However, if you will suspend your disbelief, you will arrive at the very essence of Persian poetry and Persian culture, where sudden mysterious appearances of the Divine are a reality, and where, six hundred years after the fact, this tongue continues to reveal divine mysteries—to sing, inspire, and transform. As Hafiz says:

> My verse is the crowning gold of creation;
> the great ones acknowledge the alchemy of this cooper.

Peter Booth
Chevy Chase, MD 2019

GLOSSARY
by Peter Booth

Beloved. The personification of God by endowing Him/Her with perceivable attributes such as beauty, coquettishness, elegance, grace, love, and compassion. In Hafiz, the Beloved has the attributes of both masculine and feminine beauty; and the third-person singular, when used to refer to the Beloved, can be read as masculine, feminine, or both, depending on the context.

Breeze. Plays the role of messenger in Hafiz's poetry. Most frequently, it is the morning breeze from the northeast that carries a message between the Beloved and lover after a night of supplication. The arrival of this message from the Beloved indicates the lover's advancement to a higher spiritual state of greater intimacy.

Candle. Well suited to Hafiz's imagery as it is an individual light whose existence depends on its own annihilation—that is, to light itself the candle burns down into nothing, as does the lover, on fire from his love for the Beloved. Over and over in Hafiz, the light of the candle/lover is seen being consumed by the dawn light of the Sun/Beloved, signifying God-realization.

Cup, Wine Cup. *See also* **Jamshid's Cup.** Just as a shell is necessary to create and carry a pearl, so, too, the wine cup or goblet is necessary to contain the wine representing Divine Love. Moreover, as all of Hafiz's imagery is "open ended," with images flowing into and expanding the meaning of one another, the wine cup, throughout his poetry and Persian history, represents the pure heart of the lover, where not just the face of the Beloved can be reflected as in a mirror, but where all of creation and all events—past, present, and future—can be viewed as well.

Cupbearer. The spiritual guide; God-realized Master.

Curl. *See* **Tress.**

Cypress. Throughout Persian mystical poetry the cypress, with its tall erect stature and silvery bark, represents the impressive, upright stature of the Beloved.

Dawn. Highly symbolic in Hafiz, especially when he uses it in phrases like "last night at dawn." This symbolizes a spiritual awakening, the ultimate goal of God-realization and also an event happening out of time.

Deer, Wild Deer. In Hafiz, as in Persian poetry, a deer usually refers to the musk deer or the deer of Khotan. The musk deer is a perfect representation for the state of the lover. Driven mad by the intoxicating fragrance of its musk pod located near its navel, the musk deer runs wildly searching everywhere for the source, not realizing that the fragrance is emanating from itself.

Dervish. One of the heroes of Hafiz's poetry. Dervishes are the true, pure lovers of God, unstained by any of the hypocrisy that Hafiz attributes to the Sufis of his time.

Drunkenness. *See also* **Ruin** and **Tavern.** Although most would argue that the drunkenness in Hafiz can be either alcoholic intoxication or the intoxication of Divine Love, Hafiz makes it clear that it is the intoxication from the effects of the Wine of Divine Love that he is always referring to and not alcoholic intoxication: "It is not the intoxication of love that is in your head—get out of here. / Your intoxication is from the juice of the grape." However, Hafiz uses the language of the "everyman" as it were, to touch and draw the most common among us from our broken state toward our ultimate state of spiritual perfection.

Friend. *See* **Beloved.**

Garden. Variously refers to the Garden of Paradise or an idealized garden where the lover and Beloved, most often portrayed as a nightingale and a rose, are in ecstatic communion with one another. Unlike the tavern, the other stage for the play of the lover-Beloved relationship, the garden for the most part is free of the images of wine, intoxication, upheaval, and effacement, and instead is saturated with the beauty and fragrance of the rose and the ecstatic song of the nightingale.

Ghazal (pronounced GUH zel). An amatory poetic form of complex structure, Arabic in origin, which was used by medieval Persian poets to convey the beauty of love, both human and divine, as well the pain of separation from, and ecstatic union with, the beloved. Hafiz revolutionized the ghazal form to create a verse of spiritual revelation, which articulates the mysteries of the path to Union with God.

God-Man. *See also* **God-realization.** The total manifestation of God in human form on Earth; the direct descent of Reality into Illusion, variously known as the Avatar, the Rasool, the Christ, the Buddha, the Highest of the High, the Eternal Living Perfect Master, the Messiah, the Ancient One. Note that Hafiz, upon receiving the grace of God-realization from his Master, attained the state of Man-God, also known as a Perfect Master (as differentiated here from the realized state of the God-Man), and consciously wrote his verse from the place where Reality descends into Illusion. *See also* **Wellspring, Om Point.** For further cross-referenced variants of God-realized states, see Meher Baba's *Discourses* glossary (all editions).

God-realization, Realization, Self-realization. *See also* **God-Man.** This concept exists in the world's two great mystical traditions—Vedantic and Islamic—although both traditions debate exactly what it means. In Vedanta the term used for a God-realized soul is *Sat Guru*, while in Islamic mysticism and Hafiz various names are given to this state, *Pir-i-Moghan* (the old Zoroastrian Master), *Murshid* (the master), and *Qutub* (the pivot) being the most common. In both traditions these names signify the God-realized Master who guides others to the goal he has obtained. Through his use of imagery, Hafiz gives a beautiful articulation of the God-realized state as being the complete merging of the individual soul with the limitless existence of God as infinite Love, while the individuality of the merged soul is maintained.

Hafiz. In the Persian ghazal, usually in the final couplet, the poet addresses himself in the third-person. The name the poet uses, essentially his pen name, is called the *takhallus.*

Hem of garment. The figure of the lover holding onto the hem of the Beloved's dress, or *daaman,* is current in both Middle Eastern and Indian literature, the most common figure being the lover as a child holding on to a parent's (or the Master's) skirt as they pass through the crowded market, the bazaar of illusion.

Jamshid's Cup. The Persian New Year, Jamshed-i-Nowruz, celebrates the moment of God-realization when King Jamshed (Jamshid) looks into the goblet of wine (Jam-i-jam) in his heart and sees his image perfectly reflected. As such, the metaphor of the wine cup providing the perfect reflection of all the secrets of existence is at the very basis of Persian culture. This metaphor, more than anything else, establishes Iranian culture as mystical in its essence.

Khidr (Khizr). The "Green One." In Sufi tradition, he is the Eternal Life Prophet, illuminated directly by God. Widely known as the guide of Moses, Khidr symbolizes the inner guide of reality for all who walk the mystical path. Meher Baba stated that during the night that Saint Francis received the stigmata of Christ's wounds at La Verna, Khidr gave the beloved saint the touch of grace, which made him a Perfect Master. *See also* **God-realization, Man-God.** (Kalchuri: 14, 5011)

Lily. Its petals shaped like tongues, it represents the tongue of speech, specifically the tongue of the lover who sings to the Beloved.

Lips. Especially the Beloved's lips, most commonly seen as kissing the Beloved's lip. Represents God-realization.

Love. In Hafiz, Love and God and the Beloved are synonymous, with these subtle differences: God is Love with the addition of idealized human qualities; the Beloved is Love with the addition of coquettish qualities.

Night. Frequently associated with dawn in Hafiz's poetry, suggesting not just that night ends in the dawn of a new spiritual state—in some cases even God-realization—but also that God as Love exists out of the framework of time.

Nightingale. Represents the lover or, in Hafiz, the tongue of the Beloved, who, inspired by the Beloved's beauty (represented by the rose), sings in joyous ecstasy.

Ocean. Used variously in Hafiz with three meanings: the limitless existence of the Beloved as Love, the vast expanse of the spiritual path, and also the vastness of creation.

Path. Refers to the spiritual path characterized by ascending states of consciousness and terminating in Union with the Beloved or God-realization.

Pearl. Represents the God-realized soul. This state of eternal unique individuality is achieved only after the soul passes through the shell of the illusion of creation. Hafiz's poetry is such a perfect representation of this process, and such a perfect representation of creation as the shell that produces the pearl, that many just see the shell and the mother of pearl without ever catching a glimpse of, or imagining that there is, a pearl hidden inside.

Reed. In Persian mysticism, the reed symbolizes the soul of the lover or artist being emptied through gradual effacement by the Beloved. Once the lover is completely hollow, the Beloved then takes him to His lips and plays the tune of divine inspiration through his being.

Rose. Represents the Beloved.

Ruin. *See also* **Drunkenness** and **Tavern.** Most often refers to the state of the lover in the tavern. The tavern is an imaginary place where spiritual advancement takes place through the destruction or ruin of one station along the spiritual path and the eventual replacement of it with a higher station. This upheaval or ruin occurs when the Beloved or God-realized Master, portrayed as the tavern keeper, dispenses the wine of Divine Love to his customers. This wine, being infinite, naturally uproots the finite until the finite completely passes away into infinity. The image of the ruin of the tavern, and the image of the drunken lover in it, is the reason Hafiz is so often misread as a poet celebrating the debauchery of drunkenness and corporeal love. Instead, however, Hafiz is using his mastery of this imagery to touch the most worldly and forsaken. Having touched them with the beauty of his verse, he then draws them toward forming the pearl of God-realization through the process described above.

Secret. The secret always was, is, and will remain a secret.

Ship. Frequently compared or related to a wine goblet, with each carrying the goods of God-realization—the wine in the goblet represents Divine Love, and Hafiz's poetry on the ship represents the spiritual guidance that can transform the reader into an eternal, unique pearl.

Shiraz. Cradled by purple-brown mountains on all sides, Hafiz's beloved, ancient garden city with its blue domes, dark cypresses, and orange groves was once called the "hub of the universe," and was known in his time for its arts and letters, saints, roses, and wine. Shiraz was spared the ravages of invading Mongols and Tartars during this chaotic period of history when its local ruler offered tributes and submission to Genghis Khan, and later Shah Shuja agreed to submit to Tamerlane. Hafiz was born, lived most of his life, and is buried in Shiraz.

Simurgh. A gigantic mythical bird, sometimes equated with a phoenix, that appears throughout Iranian art and literature. It lives in the Tree of Knowledge and possesses benevolent and healing qualities. In Farid al-Din Attar's *Conference of the Birds*, a band of birds led by the hoopoe sets out on a quest to find the simurgh.

Sky. Best translated as the "empyrean," with all of its rich connotations of the highest heaven, the stratosphere. Hafiz frequently refers to the sky as "the dome," to stress, perhaps, its curvature, as in Hafiz, curvature is what brings about creation from the perfectly erect stature of God as Love.

Slave. In Hafiz, slavery equals freedom. Being the slave of the Boundless One grants freedom from the shackles and bindings of illusion.

Street. Best translated as "lane" or "back alleyway," the area around where the Beloved lives, or the area where the Beloved, as the figurative tavern keeper, or *Saki*, has his tavern. To enter into the Beloved's street or lane is to enter into the realm of real spirituality. It is not possible to enter the Beloved's lane without humility.

Sufism. A mystical branch of Islam with a focus on the direct experience of the Divine. Hafiz, however, most often refers to Sufis as hypocrites as the Sufi orders during his time were taken over by false masters.

Sun. Variously seen as the standard symbol for the source of light, love, and compassion, but also portrayed as being insignificant in comparison to the effulgence of God-realization, the end product of the soul's passage through the darkness of creation.

Tavern. *See also* **Drunkenness** and **Ruin.** Historically, in Iran, dilapidated structures of gambling and prostitution located on the edge of cities and run by the Zoroastrians. While alcohol was forbidden to Muslims, in Hafiz's time the taverns were tolerated for their substantial tax revenues. In traditional mystical poetry, taverns symbolize man's ruined state after his fall from paradise. The tavern is also a metaphorical spiritual state where man's lower self is annihilated or ruined in order for his true existence as God to manifest.

Tulip. Represents a wine goblet. The black spot in the bottom of its blossom represents the sorrow it feels from being separated from the Beloved, but its wine-goblet shape allows it to contain the metaphorical intoxicating liquid or "wine" of Divine Love. As is exemplified here, and in all of Hafiz's imagery, there is both the pain of separation accompanied by a sense of the redemption or salvation of Union.

Tress, Hair, Curl. In general, Hafiz uses the Beloved's tresses or curls as chains that trap and bind the lover's heart. Elsewhere, however, they are the spiraling ascending curves of the spiritual path with all of its twists and turns. The most common setting involving curls is the bird of the soul or the heart, attracted by the beauty mark on the Beloved's cheek, becoming caught in them. These bindings then draw the heart/soul from illusion to Reality represented by the Beloved's cheek and His/Her lips.

Union. The ultimate state of lover and Beloved. The Persian mystics presented the allegory that every particle of man was composed of dust and the wine of God's love carefully kneaded by the angels under God's instructions over a forty-day period. This process expressed the descent of man's soul into the chalice of God's covenant—the human form. It is the undoing of this process (the spiritual path) that is the ascension of man's soul back to its source with God. This culmination is termed Union with God, or God-realization. The unfoldment to Union is the subject of Hafiz's poetry.

Veil. In mystical traditions, a covering over the human eye. One remains "veiled" until such time as, by the grace of a God-realized Master, the soul sees the divine effulgence of God. In Islam, the veil hiding the radiance of the Divine is composed of seventy thousand layers of light and darkness.

Wellspring, Om Point. Where Hafiz positioned himself and wrote, "Ultimately the aspirant has to realize that God is the only Reality and that he is really one with God. This implies that he should not be overpowered by the spectacle of the multiform universe. In fact, the whole universe is in the Self and springs into existence from the tiny point in the Self, referred to as the Om Point. But the Self as the individualized soul has become habituated to gathering experiences through one medium or another, and therefore it comes to experience the universe as a formidable rival, other than itself. Those who have realized God constantly see the universe as springing from this Om Point, which is in everyone" (Meher Baba, *Discourses*, 190).

Zikr (pronounced ZI ker). The repetition of God's name, attributes, or short phrases from the hadith or the Qur'an, as a devotional practice to glorify God and achieve spiritual intoxication.

❦ ACKNOWLEDGMENTS ❦

Concerned that we might miss the mark in assembling Hafiz's illumined work into a coherent and authentic collection for today, signs of reassurance and unexpected generosity from all directions kept us buoyant and grateful. For us (Michael and Saliha), this work has been a fragrant remembrance of the thirteen years we spent with our teacher, the great Sufi saint His Holiness M. R. Bawa Muhaiyaddeen—may love surround him. Simply sitting with this small, exquisite "ant man" (as he called himself), someone who was empty of self and filled with love, illuminated our way with grace.

For me (Nancy), it was 1995 when Hafiz's arrow first pierced my heart in the form of renderings of his couplets taped to the Meeting Place wall at the Meher Spiritual Center. The arrow is lodged, still, and whatever my role with Hafiz's work has been through these years is due solely to Avatar Meher Baba's love for his favorite poet Hafiz, and for All.

We're deeply grateful and offer evergreen thanks to each of the primary contributors, Coleman Barks, Robert Bly, Omid Safi, Peter Booth, and Meher Baba (via the Avatar Meher Baba Trust) for their heart-filled generous gifts of permission for use of translations and commentary. Thanks for permission extend to Mehernath Kalchuri of the Bhau Kalchuri estate, and to Jonathan Granoff for his contributions and broad reach. The possibility to include more grace note excerpts opened late in the project. Our gratitude for these extend to the kindness of Carl Ernst, Thomas Rain Crowe, Elizabeth T. Gray, Jr. and Iraj Anvar, James R. Newell, Mehernoush Lorkalantari McPherson, Farshid Namiranian, Tim Campbell, and the late Annemarie Schimmel (by way of UNC Press).

The work of many other translators couldn't be included here, so we bow to those who continue to spread the incomparable verse of Hafiz that bridges time, space, cultures, and hearts. And, of course—thank you, Hafiz.

Big, warm thanks also to poet Thomas R. Smith, for assistance with Robert Bly's work; to Frederick T. Courtright of The Permissions Company, for his Jedi mastery of rights and ever-ready help; to Larry and Cathy Didona, for loving design and standby; to Charlie Mills, for the generous gift from your brush; Mehera Blum, for use of your beloved mom Laurie's paintings; Farid Mohammadi, for the photo of Coleman and Robert at Hafiz's tomb; and to Peter Booth, again, for giving more and still yet more.

Sincere thanks to our inspired editor Jennifer Y. Brown for being such a great traveling companion; Brian Galvin, VP of sales, for his love of Hafiz and belief in this project; to publisher Tami Simon for her vision; to Sounds True team Jennifer Miles, Anastasia Pellouchoud, Lindsey Kennedy, Christine Day, Amy Sinopoli, Jade Lascelles, Beth Skelley, Jill Rogers, Samantha Sacks, and all, for great aim at a moving target.

Nancy gives thanks and love always to my husband Knight, sons Thatcher and Owen, and daughter-in-law Jessica; to Mom and Dad, my sister Jayne, brother David, and my extended family, for support during years spent with Hafiz. Thanks to best old friends Mitty, Mike and Irina Beal, and Linda Reichert and Mark Putnam, for safe havens and a place to keep working on this book during Hurricane Florence and floods. Gratitude always to Bhau Kalchuri for his mandali-model of love and service, and to Janice Rieman, Lynwood Sawyer, Joanna Tompkin, and Shaheen Khorshandi. Thanks to Daniel Ladinsky, for opening the door with his work in the spirit of Hafiz; to Zo Newell; Janet, Bill and Gordy-the-Om-dog Files; Cherie Cooper; Bahram Namiranian; David Fenster; Jean Tresselt; Denny Moore; Marjan Namiranian; Doug Cox, Rita Connie; Joe Dunn, Sher Dimaggio, Tony Zois, Ellen Kimball; Charlie Gard'ner; Sally and David Katz; and Martha Marmouze, for all sorts of kindness.

Saliha and Michael send love to Kaleo and Kai, for the glory of being young; their parents Ani and Kabir; and Chuck and George, who first showed us Isfahan. Deepest thanks to the Bawa Muhaiyaddeen Fellowship and Funny Family for the wellspring of pure wisdom. For their inspiration and generosity, our gratitude goes to Jonathan (Ahamed) and Moon Granoff, and Dana and Rose Hayne. Special appreciation to all those who appear in the book or graciously lent their art: Rob Smith, for raising his arms; Myra Diaz, for splendid calligraphy; Gary Elliot, for glimpses of Baisha Village; Hamida Toomey, for resting in light; John and Maryam Cucci, for Sufi falconry; Sayyid Salman Chisti, for joy; Kate Zaia Grace Czaja, for rowing into luminance; Zena Stein, for a life full of caring; The Illumination Band, for joining two worlds: Kabir, David, Jeff, Bill, Steve, Shams, Amira, and honorary members Ilmi, Sam, Knight, Peter, Owen, Thatcher, Michael K., and Brian W. (whirledmusic.org); the sister angels: Elisabet, Marie, Sue, Ruthie, Lizzy, Brenda, Betsy, and Dana; all the Peaceable Friends: Na'im, Chuck G., Chuck C., Ed S., Wick, Abu Bakr, Atesh, Salihu, Ed K., Chris, Tony, Locke, Jonathan, George, Jody, Michael T., and Albert. And we're forever grateful to Leslie Gignilliat-Day and Tim Campbell at Amber Lotus Publishing for introducing us to Hafiz.

⚜ About the Contributors ⚜

Art and Design

MICHAEL GREEN is a fine artist who has devoted his skills to creating works that evoke the contemplative and sacred traditions. He is the illustrator of the long-bestselling *The Illuminated Rumi* with Coleman Barks, *The Illuminated Prayer, The Unicornis Manuscripts*, and many other books. He has created art and experiential sculpture gardens for hospitals and healing gardens around the country, including the Children's Discovery Garden at the Lucile Packard Children's Hospital Stanford. He lives with his wife Saliha in Pennsylvania. Together, they host concerts and art shows at the Green Barn Studios. His current projects include *The Afterculture* and *A New Book of Kells*. Visit him at michaelgreenarts.com.

SALIHA GREEN studied fine art at Mount Holyoke College, horticulture at The Barnes Arboretum School and Longwood Gardens, and combined these arts as a native plant garden designer. She is the director of The Glen Rose Conservancy, dedicated to protecting the local Brandywine watershed. In 2005, Saliha began creating images to accompany the verses of Hafiz for Amber Lotus PublishIng. Her next projects include illustrating children's books with themes of spirituality, mindfulness, beauty, and environmental protection. Visit her at salihagreen.com.

Translations and Commentary

MEHER BABA (1894–1969) was born in India of Persian Zoroastrian parents. A world spiritual figure, Avatar Meher Baba often highlighted his discourses and conversations with the verse of his favorite poet, saying, "Hafiz says it best." Meher Baba's life of love, supremely lived, and his perfect mastery in servitude personified humanity's potential to live a divine life on earth. In 1925, he initiated arrangements for the restoration of Hafiz's tomb and nearby gardens, and from this year also until his passing, he maintained complete silence despite his vast scope of work that included extensive humanitarian activities and world travels. Primary titles among his many books are *God Speaks* and *Discourses*. To learn more, visit ambppct.org.

COLEMAN BARKS is an internationally renowned poet and translator and the bestselling author of *The Essential Rumi, Rumi: The Big Red Book, The Soul of Rumi,* and numerous other titles of original poetry and translations including *The Illuminated Rumi* with Michael Green. He was predominantly featured in two of Bill Moyers' PBS television series, *The Language of Life* and *Fooling with Words*. In 2006, he received an honorary doctorate at the University of Tehran for his years of work with Rumi. Barks taught English and poetry at the University of Georgia for thirty years and now focuses on writing, readings, and performances. Visit him at colemanbarks.com.

ROBERT BLY is a poet, author, translator, activist, and leader of the international mythopoetic men's movement for which his renowned title *Iron John: A Book about Men* was a key text that remained on the *New York Times* Best Sellers List for sixty-two weeks. Inspired by a broad range of spiritual traditions, Bly has profoundly affected American verse, introducing many unknown European and South American poets as well as little-known Middle Eastern poets to new readers. His awards include the Poetry Society of America's Frost Medal, the National Book Award, and two Guggenheims. His recent *Collected Poems* gathers together fourteen volumes of his work to showcase his monumental poetic achievement. Visit him at robertbly.com.

PETER BOOTH is a Hafiz scholar and translator and the coauthor of *Dante / Hafiz.* He studied Sanskrit and sacred Indian texts at Georgetown University in his teens, received a BA in English from Bard College, and attended Harvard Graduate School in Persian language and literature, studying with Annemarie Schimmel and Wheeler Thackston. He then studied Persian literature at Ferdowsi University of Mashhad, on a scholarship from the Shah of Iran. For thirty-two years he was a resident in Avatar Meher Baba's home, Meherabad, in rural India. He is currently completing a detailed study of the poetry of Hafiz titled *The Incomparable Hafiz.*

OMID SAFI, PhD, is a professor of Asian and Middle Eastern studies at Duke University. He's an American Muslim public intellectual of Iranian heritage who speaks frequently in major media on the intersection of liberation and spirituality. He serves on the board of the Pluralism Project at Harvard University and is invested in the Sufi tradition, the legacy of Malcolm X, and Martin Luther King Jr. His works include *Memories of Muhammad, Radical Love,* and a forthcoming book on Rumi. He is a regular contributor to *On Being with Krista Tippett* and has a podcast at *Be Here Now.* He directs an adult education program in Turkey and Morocco, open to all. To learn more, visit illuminatedtours.com.

JONATHAN GRANOFF is an international lawyer, scholar, and award-winning screenwriter who serves as president of the Global Security Institute, representative to the UN of the Permanent Secretariat of the World Summit of Nobel Peace Laureates, and ambassador for Peace, Security and Nuclear Disarmament of The Parliament of the World's Religions. He serves on the boards of the Bawa Muhaiyaddeen Fellowship, Universal Sufi Council, Tikkun, International Association of Sufism, and Parliamentarians for Nuclear Nonproliferation and Disarmament working to bring the values of love, compassion, and justice into action. He is a fellow in the World Academy of Arts and Science and was nominated for the Nobel Peace Prize in 2014. Visit him at gsinstitute.org.

Editor

NANCY OWEN BARTON is a literary agent and editor, and also serves on the publishing team for the estate of Indian author Bhau Kalchuri. She is a contributor to *The Purity of Desire:100 Poems of Rumi* by Daniel Ladinsky, and to his *Darling, I Love You!* with Patrick McDonnell. A former professional dancer and arts educator, performance venues included Lincoln Center, Symphony Space, and Mandali Hall in India. She conducted dance research and taught in China, developed early childhood literacy and arts programs for the state of North Carolina, and served on the faculties of the National Institutes of Health POPI School and St. Andrew's School in Delaware. Visit her at nobaliterary.com.

🔺 Sources and Permissions 🔺

All translations and text from the contributors' copyrighted works, listed below, as well as any changes that appear herein, are used by permission. Hafiz did not title his verse. Titles of poems that contributors gave to their translations are noted in the Index of Sources by First Lines. Indexed lines stating "from" indicate an excerpt.

MEHER BABA *The Everything and the Nothing* by Meher Baba. (Ahmednagar, India: Avatar Meher Baba Perpetual Public Charitable Trust [AMBPPCT], 1989). First published and copyright © 1963 by Meher House Publications, Beacon Hill, Australia. Copyright © 1989 by AMBPPCT and used with permission. ambppct.org.

_____. *Lord Meher: The Biography of the Avatar of the Age Meher Baba* by Bhau Kalchuri. (Ahmednagar, India: Avatar Meher Baba Perpetual Public Charitable Trust [AMBPPCT], 2003). Translated from Hindi and original copyright © 1971 by Bhau Kalchuri. First published by Manifestation Inc. as a 20-volume edition 1986–2001. Original online edition, fwb104.org. Revised, expanded online edition, lordmeher.org. Lord Meher copyright © 2003 by AMBPPCT. Used by permission of AMBPPCT in consultation with Mehernath Kalchuri.

COLEMAN BARKS *The Hand of Poetry: Five Mystic Poets of Persia,* lectures by Inayat Khan, translations by Coleman Barks (New Lebanon: Omega Publications, 1993). Translations and introduction copyright © 1993 by Coleman Barks and used with his permission. Visit him at colemanbarks.com.

ROBERT BLY *The Angels Knocking on the Tavern Door: Thirty Poems of Hafez,* translated by Robert Bly and Leonard Lewisohn (New York: HarperCollins, 2008, first ed.). Copyright © 2008 by Robert Bly and used with his permission. Visit him at robertbly.com.

PETER BOOTH *Dante / Hafiz: Readings on the Gaze, the Sigh, and Beauty* by Franco Masciandaro and Peter Booth (Middletown: KAF Press, 2017). Hafiz translations copyright © 2017 by Peter Booth and used with his permission.

_____. *The Incomparable Hafiz* (forthcoming). Copyright © 2019 by Peter Booth and used with his permission.

TIM CAMPBELL *Night Light,* 2nd edition. Copyright © 2019 by Tim Campbell and used with his permission.

THOMAS RAIN CROWE *Drunk on the Wine of the Beloved: 100 Poems of Hafiz,* translated by Thomas Rain Crowe (Boston: Shambhala, 2001). Copyright © 2001 by Thomas Rain Crowe and used with his permission. Visit him at newnative.wordpress.com.

CARL W. ERNST, PhD *The Shambhala Guide to Sufism* (Boston: Shambhala, 1997). Copyright © 1997 by Carl W. Ernst and used with his permission. Visit him at religion.unc.edu/_people/full-time-faculty/ernst/.

JONATHAN GRANOFF *Practical Mysticism.* Copyright © 2018 by Jonathan Granoff and used with his permission. Visit him at gsinstitute.org/who-we-are/.

ELIZABETH T. GRAY, JR. and IRAJ ANVAR *Wine & Prayer: Eighty Ghazals from the Diwan of Hafiz* (Ashland: White Cloud Press, 1995). Translation copyright © 1995 by Elizabeth T. Gray Jr. and Iraj Anvar and used with their permission. Visit them at elizabethtgrayjr.com, vivo.brown.edu/display/ianvar.

MEHERNOUSH LORKALANTARI Verse translated directly and used with her permission.

FARSHID NAMIRANIAN Verse relayed from memory and used with his permission.

JAMES R. NEWELL "Heartbroken Nightingale" excerpt from *The Songs of Hafiz,* CD, Copyright © 2016 by James R. Newell and used with his permission. Visit him at thesongsofhafiz.com.

OMID SAFI *Radical Love: Teachings from the Islamic Mystical Tradition*, translated and edited by Omid Safi (New Haven: Yale University Press, 2018). Copyright © 2018 by Omid Safi and used by permission of the translator and Yale University Press. Visit him at illuminatedtours.com.

ANNEMARIE SCHIMMEL *A Two-Colored Brocade: The Imagery of Persian Poetry* (Chapel Hill: The University of North Carolina Press, 1992). Copyright © 1992 by UNC Press and used with permission.

✦ INDEX OF SOURCES BY FIRST LINE ✦

Robert and Coleman at Hafiz's tomb in Shiraz, Iran

☗ Illustration Credits ☗

All photos, paintings, and images are used by permission.

☗ Select Bibliography ☗

The following titles are included to offer readers a broader understanding of Hafiz's verse, his life and times, and the spiritual, inner unfoldment of *the path of love*. Where there are multiple or earlier editions we refer to the title we had at hand while shaping this book.

Arberry, A. J. *Shiraz: Persian City of Saints and Poets.* Norman: University of Oklahoma Press, 1960.
Attar, Farid-ud Din. *The Conference of the Birds: A Sufi Fable.* Translated by C. S. Nott. Boston: Shambhala, 1993.
Baqli, Ruzbihan. *The Unveiling of Secrets: Diary of a Sufi Master.* Translated by Carl W. Ernst. Chapel Hill, NC: Parvardigar Press, 1997.
Bawa Muhaiyadeen, M. R. *The Golden Words of a Sufi Sheikh.* Reprint. Philadelphia: The Fellowship Press, 2006.

_____. *A Book of God's Love.* Philadelphia: The Fellowship Press, 1994.

_____. *Questions of Life, Answers of Wisdom.* 2 vols. Philadelphia: The Fellowship Press, 1990–2000.

_____. *Dhikr: The Remembrance of God.* Philadelphia: The Fellowship Press, 1999.

Bell, Gertrude. *Poems from the Divan of Hafiz.* London: Murray, 1928.

Bly, Robert, ed. *The Soul is Here for Its Own Joy: Sacred Poems from Many Cultures.* New York: HarperCollins, 1995.

Chittick, William. *Divine Love: Islamic Literature and the Path to God.* New Haven: Yale University Press, 2013.

Emerson, Ralph Waldo. *Emerson: Collected Poems and Translations.* Edited by Harold Bloom and Paul Kane. New York: Library of America, 1994.

Ernst, Carl W. *The Shambhala Guide to Sufism.* Boston: Shambhala Publications, 1997.

_____. *Words of Ecstasy in Sufism.* Albany: SUNY, 1985.

Hafiz. *The Divan-i-Hafiz.* Translated and edited by H. Wilberforce Clarke. Reprint of 1891 edition, with a new introduction by Michael C. Hillman. Bethesda, MD: Ibex, 2007.

Hafiz. *Divan of Hafiz.* 2 vols. Translated by Paul Smith. Melbourne: New Humanity Books, 1986.

Hafiz. *Drunk on the Wine of the Beloved: 100 Poems of Hafiz.* Translated by Thomas Rain Crowe. Boston: Shambhala, 2001.

Hafiz. *Fifty Poems of Hafiz.* Translated by A. J. Arberry, et al. Cambridge: Cambridge University Press, 1962.

Hafiz. *Wine & Prayer: Eighty Ghazals from the Díwán of Háfiz.* Translated by Elizabeth T. Gray, Jr. and Iraj Anvar. Ashland, OR: White Cloud Press, 2019.

Hafiz. *The Tangled Braid: Ninety-Nine Poems by Hafiz of Shiraz.* Translated by Jeffrey Einboden and John Slater. Louisville: Fons Vitae, 2009.

Hafez. *Hafez: Translations and Interpretations of the Ghazals.* Translated by Geoffrey Squires. Oxford: Miami University Press, 2014.

Halman, Hugh Talat. *Where the Two Seas Meet: The Quranic Story of al-Khidr and Moses in Sufi Commentaries as a Model of Spiritual Guidance.* Louisville: Fons Vitae, 2013.

Kahn, Inayat. "Sufi Poetry." In *The Teaching of Hazrat Inayat Khan.* Vol. 10. Hazrat Inayat Khan Study Database Accessed January 31, 2019. hazrat-inayat-khan.org/php/views.php?h1=34&h2=7.

Inayat-Kahn, Pir Zia. *Mingled Waters: Sufism and the Mystical Unity of Religions.* New Lebanon, NY: Suluk Press/ Omega Publications, 2017.

Lewisohn, Leonard, ed. *Hafiz and the Religion of Love in Classical Persian Poetry.* New York: I. B. Tauris, 2015.

Limbert, John. *Shiraz in the Age of Hafez: The Glory of a Medieval Persian City.* Seattle: University of Washington Press, 2004.

Meher Baba. *Discourses.* 7th revised ed. Myrtle Beach, SC: Sheriar Press, 1987.

_____. *God Speaks: The Theme of Creation and Its Purpose.* New York: Dodd, Mead and Co., 1973.

_____. *The Path of Love.* Myrtle Beach, SC: Sheriar Foundation, 2000.

Nasr, Sayyed Hossein. *The Garden of Truth: The Vision and Promise of Sufism, Islam's Mystical Tradition.* Reprint, New York: HarperOne, 2008.

Newell, James R. "The Wisdom of Intoxication: Love and Madness in the Poetry of Hafiz of Shiraz." In *Creativity, Madness and Civilisation,* edited by Richard Pine, 200–215. Newcastle: Cambridge Scholars Publishing, 2007.

Pourafzal, Haleh, and Roger Montgomery. *The Spiritual Wisdom of Haféz: Teachings of the Philosopher of Love.* Rochester, VT: Inner Traditions, 1998.

Schimmel, Annemarie. *A Two-Colored Brocade: The Imagery of Persian Poetry.* Chapel Hill: The University of North Carolina Press, 1992.

Thackston, Wheeler M. *A Millennium of Classical Persian Poetry: A Guide to the Reading and Understanding of Persian Poetry from the Tenth to the Twentieth Century.* Bethesda, MD: Ibex Publishers, 1994.

About Sounds True

Sounds True is a multimedia publisher whose mission is to inspire and support personal transformation and spiritual awakening. Founded in 1985 and located in Boulder, Colorado, we work with many of the leading spiritual teachers, thinkers, healers, and visionary artists of our time. We strive with every title to preserve the essential "living wisdom" of the author or artist. It is our goal to create products that not only provide information to a reader or listener, but that also embody the quality of a wisdom transmission.

For those seeking genuine transformation, Sounds True is your trusted partner. At SoundsTrue.com you will find a wealth of free resources to support your journey, including exclusive weekly audio interviews, free downloads, interactive learning tools, and other special savings on all our titles.

To learn more, please visit SoundsTrue.com/freegifts or call us toll-free at 800.333.9185.